The Sinopedia Series

CHINA'S SCIENCE, TECHNOLOGY, AND EDUCATION

The Sinopedia Series

CHINA'S SCIENCE, TECHNOLOGY, AND EDUCATION

XI QIAOJUAN • ZHANG AIXIU

Australia • Brazil • Japan • Korea • Mexico • Singapore • Spain • United Kingdom • United States

China's Science, Technology, and Education

Xi Qiaojuan and Zhang Aixiu

Publishing Director:
Paul Tan

Editorial Manager:
Yang Liping

Associate Development Editor:
Joe Ng

Associate Development Editor:
Tanmayee Bhatwadekar

Senior Product Director:
Janet Lim

Product Managers:
Kevin Joo
Lee Hong Tan

Assistant Publishing Manager:
Pauline Lim

Production Executive:
Cindy Chai

Translators:
Lei Jing

Copy Editor:
Susan Amy

Cover Designer:
Ong Lay Keng

Compositor:
Integra Software Services,
Pvt. Ltd.

ISBN-13: 978-981-4319-81-2

ISBN-10: 981-4319-81-3

Cengage Learning Asia Pte Ltd
5 Shenton Way #01-01
UIC Building
Singapore 068808

Cengage Learning is a leading provider of customized learning solutions with office locations around the globe, including Singapore, the United Kingdom, Australia, Mexico, Brazil, and Japan. Locate your local office at: **www.cengage.com/global**

Cengage Learning products are represented in Canada by Nelson Education, Ltd.

For product information, visit **www.cengageasia.com**

Printed in Singapore
1 2 3 4 5 12 11 10

Table of Contents

The launch of the Shenzhou-7 manned spaceship.

Preface

In 2008, China witnessed two significant national events that drew global attention. One was the 29th Olympic Games, successfully held in Beijing. The International Olympic Committee (IOC) President Jacques Rogge described it as an "unprecedented" event. From the opening to the closing ceremonies, from the Olympics to the Paralympics, these "high-tech" Olympics fully displayed the country's attractions. Much of the high-tech equipment used in the Olympics was invented in Chinese universities. Examples include the panoramic intelligent simulation scheduling system, the cauldron ignition system, the fully electric-driven bus, and the dynamic fireworks during the opening ceremony.

The other event refers to the space walk of the astronauts of the Shenzhou-7 manned spaceship on September 27, making China the third country after Russia and the United States to master extravehicular space technology. This large, complex, and highly integrated manned space flight embodied the wisdom and painstaking work of thousands of scientific and technological personnel. President Hu Jintao emphasized at the celebration of the success of the mission that education should be given strategic priority and developed vigorously to lay a solid foundation for the development of creative talent.

For science and technology to develop rapidly, the popularization of science and technology can set the level of productivity and culture, and the ability of a nation to innovate. In the history of human civilization, major scientific discoveries and technological inventions have had great impacts on societies.

It is a commonly understood fact that today's international competition is focused on science and technology talent. Before 1949, the level of scientific and technological development was rather low in China. There were only about 30 specialized research institutions and less than 50,000 science and technology personnel. Primary school enrolment was only 20% while illiteracy rate was as high as 80%. During the early years after the establishment of the People's Republic of China, the nation's science and technology had to be rebuilt from these dismal situations.

Hence, the Chinese government promoted the slogan of "Marching Toward Science." It also adopted a series of strategic initiatives to accelerate the development of science, technology, and education. These strategies resulted in breakthroughs in science and technology which made historic

Fireworks during the Opening Ceremony of the Beijing Olympic Games 2008.

leaps in education that quickly changed the backward state of development in these areas.

On May 24, 1977, the then paramount leader Deng Xiaoping noted that "compared with developed countries, the science, technology, and education of our country has lagged far behind for 20 years. ... We must place equal emphasis on science, technology, and education. We must strengthen these two aspects, starting from primary to middle schools, and on to universities. ... We should 'walk with both legs,' paying attention to both popularization and improvements for the launch of the Shenzhou-7 manned spaceship."

Since the reform and opening-up policies began, China has established and implemented a strategy of revitalizing the country through science, technology, and education. Development has been rapid. Consequently, the country has become a world leader in a number of areas while witnessing vigorous development in education. It has built the largest national education system in the world, laying a reliable foundation and creating the impetus to propel economic and social development forward, while enhancing national supremacy and international competitiveness.

Modern developments in these fields depend on the thorough implementation of the strategy to develop and revitalize China through science, technology, and education, which is a long-term strategy. This means giving these three fields strategic importance in the economic and social development of the country. China also aspires for advanced science and technology, a well-developed educational system, continuous knowledge innovation, and a high quality labor force that can drive and support economic and social development to achieve the objective of modernizing a socialist economy and moving toward a knowledge economy. All these have laid a solid foundation for China's peaceful rise and the nation's grand revival in the 21st century.

Chapter 1

China's Education and Her Research and Development System

China's Research and Development System

Since the 1980s, China began to focus on developing her economy and shifted from a planned economy to a socialist market economy. Policies related to her science and technology system were correspondingly adjusted. The country's research and development (R&D) system experienced institutional reform. The government-led central planning system underwent changes and a new science and technology system gradually took shape.

The new system is based on the idea that economic growth should rely on science and technology, and that scientific and technological work must be oriented toward economic growth. Features of the system include a clear division of labor and a mutually supportive relationship among state-owned scientific and technological institutes, industry research departments, and institutions of higher learning. At the same time, the system should assist private technology enterprises to grow and achieve their results rapidly.

Major Scientific Research Institutes

China's research system is mainly driven by scientific and technological efforts from state-owned R&D institutions, institutions of higher learning, and private enterprises.

State-owned R&D Institutions State-owned R&D institutions are an important driver of China's research and development. Perhaps the finest example is the Chinese Academy of Sciences (CAS). Established on November 1, 1949, this academy is not only the highest science and technology academic institution, but is also the national development center for the natural sciences and high-tech comprehensive research. A large number of China's best scientists converge in the affiliated research institutions of the Chinese Academy of Sciences. They work on basic research, social welfare research, high-tech research and development, and initiate innovations in the high-tech industry. In the past 60 years, the Chinese Academy of Sciences has achieved a series of major research results such as the Two Missiles and One Satellite Program that made great contributions to the country's science and technology development, national economic and social development, as well as her national defense.

CAS has also recruited more than over 45,000 postgraduate students and educated numerous talented technological innovators. The academy has a team of high-level scientific experts and 37,000 professional technical personnel. Of this number, 256 are academicians of the Chinese Academy of Sciences, and 53 are academicians of the Chinese Academy of Engineering.

As a national agricultural scientific research institute, the Chinese Academy of Agricultural Sciences shoulders the tasks of researching the nation's most important sector, as well as the foundation, research, and application of high-tech industries within agriculture. The academy is made up of 39 research institutes, 1 graduate school, and the China Agricultural Science and Technology Press. Among the 39 research institutes, 16 work on crop farming, 10 work on aquaculture, 8 focus on economic and environmental

FYI
FOR YOUR INFORMATION

TWO MISSILES AND ONE SATELLITE PROGRAM

The Two Missiles and One Satellite Program announced the arrival of China's cutting-edge technology in the world from the 1960s to 1970s. The program resulted in the successful production and testing of China's first atomic bomb on October 16, 1964, her first hydrogen bomb on June 17, 1967, and the successful launch of her first man-made satellite on April 24, 1970.

This picture shows a meeting between Mao Zedong and Qian Xuesen. Qian Xuesen (1911–2009) was one of the top scientists of China's Two Missiles and One Satellite Program. He was one of the pioneers of manned spaceship technology research and the founder of engineering cybernetics in China. He was the most prominent figure in applied science of the 20th century and was known as "China's Father of Space," "Father of China's Missiles," and "the King of Rockets."

The Chinese Academy of Sciences at No. 52, Sanlihe Road, Beijing.

resources, and 5 on agricultural engineering and the latest technology for agriculture. The Chinese Academy of Agricultural Sciences owns 2 state key laboratories, 20 key departmental laboratories, 6 national crop improvement centers, 27 national and departmental quality assurance centers (that also includes inspection and testing), 1 national crop germplasm resource center, 11 national crop germplasm centers (including natural resources gardens), and 26 agricultural and animal husbandry testing grounds.

The Chinese Academy of Forestry Sciences was set up in 1958. It is located at the foot of Yuquan Mountain west of Beijing. It is a comprehensive, multidisciplinary, social welfare-oriented research institute. The institute is managed directly by the State Forestry Administration. The academy consists of 12 research institutes, 3 R&D centers, and 4 forestry experimental centers spread across 11 provinces. Its major tasks include forestry-related fundamental and applied research, as well as high-tech industrial development and research. The academy also focuses on key and basic technological forestry issues to develop modern forestry platforms. Its major research fields include: forest cultivation, forest ecology, environmental protection, resource management, timber processing and utilization, chemicals, insects, forestry economics, and science and technology information.

Established in 1956, the Chinese Academy of Medical Sciences is China's only state-level academic center focused on the medical sciences. It is also a comprehensive scientific research institution. The academy is linked to the Chinese Peking Union Medical College. The two rely on and complement each other, enhancing each other's education and research competencies. In the academy, there are 18 research institutes (and two branch institutes), including those focusing on clinical research, preclinical medicine research, angiocardiopathy, medical, medical information, cancer research, pharmaceutical biological research, and microcirculation research, as well as five branch academies, seven clinical hospitals, and five colleges.

The Chinese Environmental Science Research Institute was founded on December 31, 1978, and is an affiliate of the Ministry of Environmental Protection. It has accomplished many national scientific and technological breakthroughs in the application of fundamental theories of environmental science and related high-tech R&D. The institute has an environmental science innovation system that focuses on research areas such as atmospheric environment, water resources, ecological environment, environmental engineering technology, environmental safety, and cleaner production in a circular economy. The academy has set up 4 research institutes, 2 research centers, 5 R&D institutions, and 2 technical service institutes, covering 18 subjects and 3 key ministerial-level laboratories. Its research staff includes 3 academicians of the Chinese Academy of

Electric buses were used during the 2008 Olympic Games in Beijing to provide transportation services for athletes and officials, in order to implement the concept of a green Olympics.

Engineering, 40 researchers and more than 100 PhDs. It has created an environmental science and engineering doctoral program with the Beijing Normal University, and has five master degree tracks and one postdoctoral workstation.

Other than the institutions mentioned above, there are many other state-owned R&D institutes, such as the Research Institute of Weaponry Science, the Chinese Academy of Building Research, among many others.

Institutions of Higher Learning   Similar to many other countries, research conducted by institutions of higher learning in many scientific research fields, especially in the study of fundamental theories of natural sciences and humanities, is critical to national development.

In recent years, research on applied theories has seen a rapid development in Chinese universities. Research conducted by famous universities such as Tsinghua, Peking, Zhejiang, and Fudan, has taken a leading position at home and is enjoying growing worldwide reputation.

In the process of cooperating with research institutions and enterprises elsewhere, China has formed a unique mode of development by carrying out various kinds of research in universities and then rapidly commercializing the results of such research. In other words, theory is used to solve current problems in production, and this practical experience is then used to enrich the existing theories and further research. Through this mode, competitive products are made and research results are quickly used to produce goods that the market demands.

The rise in the role and position of university research in recent years is self-evident. During the 10th Five-Year Plan period (2001–2005), state universities won a combined 75 state-level natural science awards, accounting for 55.07% of the total awards; 64 state technological invention awards, 64.4% of the total, and 433 national scientific and technological progress awards amounting to 53.57% of the total. Among these awards, one was a first prize in the natural sciences and two were first prizes in state technological invention. The latter broke a six-year long winning streak by the same institute.

Universities have played a significant role in the country's scientific and technological progress. The former Minister of Science and Technology Xu Guanhua praised universities, saying that "universities have become the main force of China's fundamental research and are an important component in applied research."

Enterprises During the planned economic period, China's research resources could be found mainly in the hands of independent research institutes. Research was conducted by independent research institutes and institutions of higher learning. With the reform of China's scientific and technological system, China's research mainstay has achieved a strategic change from independent research institutes to enterprises.

In recent years, the construction of the state's innovation system has been smooth. In particular, the dominant position of enterprises as technical innovators has become stronger and their role in driving scientific and technological progress and economic development has become increasingly apparent.

Statistics show that in 2007, 8,954 enterprises undertook experimental and development projects, accounting for 24.7% of all enterprises. Research and development expenditures among various types of enterprises amounted to RMB 268.19 billion or 72.3% of the total spent on R&D. Leading large and medium-sized industrial enterprises spent RMB 211.25 billion, accounting for 56.9% of the total spent in R&D and 16.3% higher than in 1995.

The construction of an entrepreneurial technical innovation system that focuses on building enterprise technology has been enhanced. Key state-owned industrial enterprises have set up their own technology centers. By 2007, there were 499 state-approved National Enterprise Technology Centers

This picture shows the R&D Center of ZTE (Zhong Xing Telecommunication Equipment Co. Ltd.) based in Nanjing.

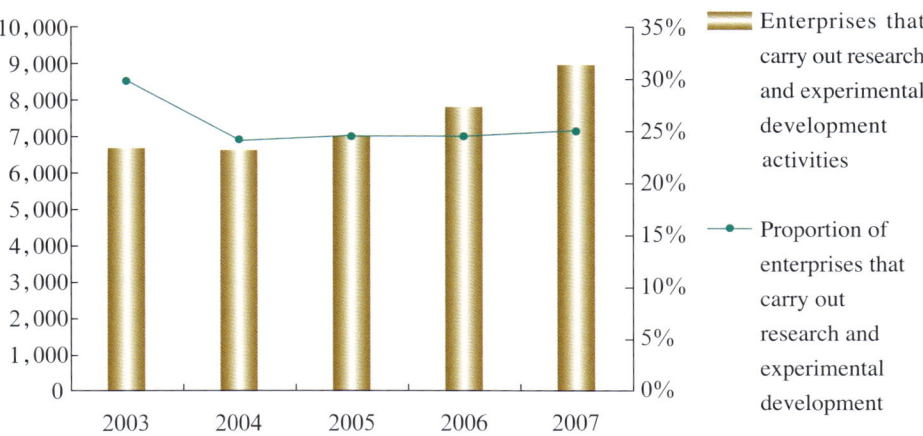

Source: *China Statistical Yearbook (2008)*

Proportion of enterprises engaged in R&D (2003–2007)

and 4,023 centers approved by the provincial governments. In 2007, state-approved technology centers were granted over RMB 80 billion for R&D, while sales of new products topped RMB 2 trillion. These numbers underscore the continuous improvement of the innovation capacity of China's enterprises.

The Technology Innovation Fund for small and medium-sized science and technology-oriented enterprises is a special government fund approved by the State Council to support the technological innovations of small and medium-sized enterprises. Since its inception in June 1999, the fund has disbursed more than RMB 7 billion, with RMB 1.26 billion spent in 2007 alone. The innovation fund has played an active role in building a favorable environment for the innovation and development of small and medium-sized technology enterprises.

Reform of Scientific Research Institutes

To adapt to China's systemic reforms, research institutes are making reforms and have achieved preliminary results. The reform of China's research institutes focuses on industry-oriented research institutes and non-profit research institutes.

Industry-oriented Research Institutes   In 1999, 242 research institutes across 10 industrial sectors under the control of the State Council carried out systemic reforms. After these reforms, the institutes were allowed to choose their own specific structure, such as a research-oriented enterprise, a fully or partially self-owned enterprise, or a technical services and intermediary organization. For the minority of research institutes that were approved by the State Council to maintain their public institution status, an operating system of technological enterprises was introduced. All 242 institutes managed to complete their reforms by end 2000.

The 242 industry-oriented institutes directly under the central government were restructured in 1999. Some of these began moving toward joint-stock reform and raised more funds by listing on public stock exchanges. A large number of listed companies with the word "science" at the beginning of their name emerged from the re-organization of those institutes. Knowledge and capital became more tightly integrated. Former "directors" became "chairmen" or "general managers." The market became the key factor in determining the development orientation and scale of science and technology.

Local development research institutes are now undergoing a similar process. These institutes are gradually completing industrial and commercial

LENOVO'S R&D CENTER IN CHINA

Located in the Shangdi High-tech Industrial Park in Haidian District, Beijing, Lenovo's China R&D Center is the core of Lenovo's global R&D system. It has staff with extensive experience in consumer product design, who are product experts in various other fields. Corporate R&D institutions such as the Lenovo Research Institute, Innovative Design Center, and various divisional R&D centers such as Lenovo Mobile, Laptops and Peripherals Research Center, as well as the Lenovo China Innovation Center all create a centralized network. The R&D hub of Lenovo China is an industry leader in IT innovations such as frame and system design for next generation personal computer devices, information security technology, collaborative computing technology, innovative design, and user research.

Datang Telecom Technology and Industry Group was established by the China Academy of Telecommunications Technology in 1999.

registration and incorporation. About half of the provincial development research institutes have completed their reforms and restructuring. Based on this transformation from institutes to enterprises, research institutes in Jiangsu, Zhejiang, Ningxia, Chongqing, Qingdao, Shenyang, Wuhan, Guangzhou, and Hangzhou have made use of corporate restructuring to operate as a more modern enterprise system.

Reform of the Nonprofit Social Research Institutes   When research institutes are transformed into enterprises, some of them can be categorized as nonprofit social research institutes. This reform was started in 2001. To date, 94% of the total nonprofit social research institutes in 18 sectors have set out to implement their reform plans.

The results of reforms in 248 such institutes are as follows: 89 institutes (36%) are managed as nonprofit research institutes under state support, and 61 institutes (25%) have been completely transformed into enterprises. The remainder (39%) have been incorporated into universities, or converted into other types of public institutions and intermediaries.

Science and Technology Administration

China's model of management for scientific and technological development is highly centralized. Within the model, the Chinese government centralizes within specific departments, the management of scientific and technological research as well as the production and allocation of resources. Other sectors are responsible for formulating and implementing the corresponding policies and short-term projects.

The scientific and technological management structure is divided into three levels. The highest decision-making organ is the National Science and Technology Education Leadership Group. One level down is the executives and coordinating staff of the Ministry of Science and Technology, other ministries, and local science and technology management units. The third level includes the management of specific scientific research institutes (colleges and universities, research institutes, enterprises, and so on).

National Science and Technology Education Leadership Group   In 1998, the State Council set up the National Science and Technology Education Leadership Group headed by Premier Zhu Rongji. Currently, the group is led by Premier Wen Jiabao and the deputy head is State Councilor Chen Zhili. The group members include

- the Director of the National Development and Reform Commission;
- the Minister of Education;

- the Minister of Science and Technology;
- the Minister of Industry and Information Technology;
- the Minister of Finance;
- the Minister of Agriculture;
- the President of the Chinese Academy of Sciences;
- the President of the Chinese Academy of Engineering;
- the Deputy Secretary-General of the State Council;
- the Director of the National Natural Science Foundation of China; and
- the Party Secretary of the China Association of Science and Technology.

The main objectives of the National Science and Technology Education Leadership Group are to

- study and review strategies and major policies on the development of science, technology, and education,
- discuss and review significant tasks and projects on science, technology, and education, and
- coordinate important events that involve science, technology, and education across State Council departments, and between central and local departments.

Under the National Science and Technology Education Leadership Group, an office has been established within the State Council General Office to handle the daily administrative matters of the group.

Ministry of Science and Technology The Ministry of Science and Technology is a government department through which the State Council centralizes and coordinates scientific and technological work. The major responsibilities of the Ministry of Science and Technology are as follows:

- to study and put forward macro strategies on the development of science and technology as well as principles, policies, and regulations on using science and technology to facilitate economic and social development;
- to study significant issues on using science and technology to facilitate economic and social development;
- to study and determine the plan and priorities of scientific and technological development,
- to promote the building of a national scientific and technological innovation system to enhance the nation's capability in this area;
- to organize and draw up long-term programs and annual plans for the development of national science and technology for the non-military sector;
- to study and formulate policies and measures on strengthening fundamental research and high-tech development;

- to take charge of plans on major fundamental research, high-tech research, and tackling key problems in science, technology, and building national scientific and technological capability;
- to strengthen high-tech industrialization and the development and promotion of applied technologies,
- to study the rational allocation of scientific research staff and to put forward policies on bringing scientific and technological initiatives from these personnel into full play, thus creating a suitable environment for their development;
- to promote the popularization of science and technology; and
- to study and draw up principles and policies for China's cooperation and exchange with foreign countries.

Other Ministries and Departments The National Development and Reform Commission, the Ministry of Education, the Ministry of Agriculture, the Ministry of Health, and the Ministry of Industry and Information Technology all participate in technology management.

This picture, taken on December 15, 2008, shows the Minister of Science and Technology Wan Gang attending the 20th Annual General Meeting. It was held to commemorate the National Torch Program.

For example, the National Development and Reform Commission is entrusted with important technology management functions, such as

- to ensure a balance in linking up social undertakings such as science and technology, education, culture, and health with national defense and national economic and social development;
- to boost the industrialization of major high-tech results;
- to work out policies on the coordinated development and mutual promotion of the economy and society; and
- to harmonize major problems in the development of various social undertakings.

The Ministry of Education cooperates with the Ministry of Science and Technology to work out principles, policies, and development plans for national-level fundamental research. It also makes plans and instructions for natural science and philosophy, and social science research in colleges and universities. It provides macro-level guidance on colleges' and universities' applied research, the promotion of high-tech, and transformation of scientific research results. Furthermore, the ministry coordinates and instructs the colleges' and universities' implementation of major national scientific research projects and research programs on national defense. Additionally, it guides the development and construction of key national laboratories and engineering research centers in colleges and universities.

The science and technology management system also involves the National Natural Science Foundation of China, the Chinese Academy of Sciences, the Chinese Academy of Engineering, and the China Association of Science and Technology. The China Association of Science and Technology is a mass organization for scientific and technical workers. It has developed into a scientific organization with 168 national societies (associations and research associations), which are divided according to the disciplines of the natural sciences, technological science, engineering and related sciences, and also includes societies that aim to boost and popularize scientific and technological development, along with 31 provincial scientific associations, and a wide range of local and grassroots organizations.

The Reform of the Education System

Elementary to Vocational Education

The continuous consolidation of results, deepened reforms, improved quality, and fast development have led to new achievements in the reform and development of education in China. These factors have contributed to the country's modernization drive and her economic and social development.

In terms of elementary education, China applies a nine-year compulsory education system that includes primary and junior secondary education. There are two types of primary school education: a five-year program and a six-year program. Similarly, there are two types of junior high school education: a three-year program and a four-year program.

Junior high school graduates can take part in the standardized examination organized by local education departments before entering senior middle school. Senior high school education takes another three years.

Rural Education Has Undergone Profound Changes and the "Two Basics" Have Seen Effective Consolidation and Improvement The Chinese government attaches great importance to rural education. During the 10th Five-Year Plan period, the State Council convened the National Conference on Basic Education and the National Rural Education Conference, and defined the most important strategic position of rural education. The state successively implemented and promulgated a series of major projects and policies to accelerate the development of rural education. Some examples include the National Project of Compulsory Education in Poor Areas, the Renovation of Dilapidated Buildings in Rural Primary and Secondary Schools, the Program for Tackling the "Two Basics"[1] in the Western Regions. These projects improved the condition of schools providing basic education in China's rural areas, especially poverty-stricken areas, and greatly eased some of the problems that students from poor families in rural areas faced. At the end of 2005, the State Council decided to reform the mechanism of funding for rural compulsory education, thoroughly bringing the funds needed for developing rural compulsory education into the scope of public financial security.

By the end of 2007, the number of counties, cities, and districts included in the universal education plan totaled 3,022,[2] accounting for 98.5% of the total population. At the same time, the "Two Basics" program covered 99% of the total population. In 2007, the total number of students attending school was 105,640,000 and the net enrollment rate of school-age children in primary school reached 99.49% of the total population. The number of junior school students in school was 57,361,900 with a gross enrollment rate of 98% of the total population. Preschool education further developed and the number of children in kindergartens (preschool classes

---

[1] The "Two Basics" focuses on implementing nine years of compulsory education and eliminating illiteracy among youths.
[2] This included 205 county-level administrative divisions.

Since the spring of 2007, all educational tuition fees have been exempted in rural schools. Students from poor rural families receive free textbooks and living allowances. This picture shows students from poor families receiving their free textbooks provided by the state. They are from Quetang Town Middle School, Xinshao County, Hunan Province.

included) totaled 23,488,300. National education and special education continue to develop at a steady pace.

Increased Development of Secondary Vocational Education and Expansion of Senior Secondary Education   During the 10th Five-Year Plan period, the State Council held two conferences on national vocational education and defined the guiding principle for schools as "Service as the Aim, Employment as the Orientation." This marked a shift from a planned system to a socialist market economy; from direct government management to regulation at the macro level, from the traditional academic-oriented role of education to one that was employment-oriented. Closely focusing on moving toward industrialization and resolving the issues concerning agriculture, countryside, and farmers, the state vigorously carried out the programs on cultivating and training skilled personnel in vocational schools for jobs in demand in the manufacturing and services sectors, and the diversion and training of the rural labor force.

During the 10th Five-Year Plan period, some 403,467,200 students went through various non-diploma training programs, at a rate of about 80,690,000 per year. By 2007, there were 14,382 secondary vocational schools (including regular specialized secondary schools, vocational high schools, technical schools, and adult specialized secondary schools). A total of 19,870,100 students attended these schools.

Senior middle school education has expanded rapidly in terms of scale and enrollment. During the 10th Five-Year Plan period, the number of students in senior high schools doubled. By 2007, there were 31,225 schools focusing on senior middle school education (including senior high schools, adult high schools, and secondary vocational schools). The number of students totaled 45,274,900, and the gross enrollment rate of senior high school reached 66%.

Comprehensive Improvement in the Quality of Schools and the Strengthening of Moral Education The national promotion of a higher quality of education has achieved major breakthroughs after years of progress. It has achieved some positive results.

This picture shows the 2009 National Vocational Skills Competition in progress.

The major measures include:

1. Deepening the reform of the basic education curriculum. Since autumn 2005, the first grade of primary schools and junior middle schools in 31 provinces, autonomous regions, and municipalities adopted new courses, while the curriculum reform of senior middle schools was carried out in four pilot provinces and regions.
2. Strengthening the training of teachers, especially rural teachers, to improve their overall quality and their capacity and ability in implementing quality education.
3. Striving to promote a balanced development of compulsory education within regions and rebuilding unqualified schools to create favorable external conditions for the implementation of quality education.

In the meantime, the plan called for actively implementing the central government's plan to further strengthen and improve the development of ideology and morality among adults, and ideological and political work among university students. Efforts also focused on developing plans to improve the moral education system at universities, middle schools and primary schools, and strengthen the relevance, effectiveness, attractiveness, and appeal of moral education.

Adult Education and Distance Education

Adult training and literacy education developed vigorously. By 2007, the number of students attending various non-diploma higher education programs reached 2,528,900, with 4,126,100 completing their courses. The number of students who completed non-diploma secondary education programs was 55,548,400, with 68,108,200 students completing their studies. Nationwide, there were 178,900 technical institutes providing vocational training and 16,000 adult elementary schools. By 2007, 957,800 people throughout the country achieved literacy and another 1,037,600 people were enrolled in basic literacy programs.

In China, the development of distance education has undergone three phases. The first phase of development is related to correspondence education, which has educated many people in China but still has considerable limitations. The second phase is radio and television education that sprang up in the 1980s. This distance education mode and Central Television University enjoy a worldwide reputation. In the 1990s, with the development of information technology and networks, modern distance learning education emerged, nudging China's distance learning education into its third phase. In September 1999, Tsinghua University, Beijing University of Posts and

Telecommunications, Zhejiang University, and Hunan University gained formal approval from the Ministry of Education to be the nation's first pilot universities to provide modern distance learning education. By 2006, a total of 68 colleges and universities had been approved to carry out distance learning pilot projects.

In 2003, the State Council promulgated the "Decision on Further Strengthening Rural Education," calling for the implementation of modern distance education in rural schools to distribute equally the amount of high-quality educational resources between urban and rural areas, and to further enhance the educational quality and effectiveness of rural education. In 2004, the central government created a special fund of RMB 364 million to fund modern distance education pilot projects, develop more than 30,000 teaching CD-ROMs, over 5,000 teaching satellite receiver stations, and 380 computer classrooms in rural schools of 12 western provinces, autonomous regions, and municipalities, as well as the Xinjiang Production and Construction Corps. In April 2004, a satellite digital channel for modern distance learning in rural schools was officially launched, providing schools in vast rural areas with free resources on classroom teaching, teacher training, special education, services for agriculture, and other vital educational needs.

"211 Project," "985 Project" and the Higher Education System

In the 60 years since the founding of modern China, higher education has gone through a transformation from elite to public education. The quality of her higher education has made immense progress and is now considered world class. The government plays a major role in running the country's higher education institutions with participation from all sectors of society. Public schools and private schools are jointly developed. In terms of the hierarchy of higher education, an atmosphere of mutual promotion and coordinated development at the three levels of professional training, undergraduate, and postgraduate education has been created.

Since the mid-1990s, through the "211 Project" and the "985 Project," the strength and quality of a number of China's key universities and disciplines were further raised. This rapid and sound development of higher education has provided quality talent and knowledge to support the country's economic and social development. By 2007, there were 2,321 ordinary colleges and universities and institutions of higher learning for adults nationwide. Out of these, 1,908 were ordinary colleges and universities, and the remaining 413 were institutions of higher learning. There were 795 institutions for postgraduate education, 479 of which were colleges and universities, while the remaining 316 were research institutes.

This picture, taken on April 24, 2008, shows primary school students attending a bilingual class. The Remote Synchronized Broadcast of the Bilingual Classroom Teaching Demonstration Month (in both Chinese and Uygur languages) of Xinjiang Uygur Autonomous Region was launched in Urumqi.

The enrollment and number of students at institutions of higher education continued to increase. In 2007, the number of students enrolled in all types of higher education totaled 27 million, with a gross enrollment rate of 23%. The number of enrolled graduates reached 1,195,000. The number of undergraduates and students in general higher education and professional training schools totaled 188.49 million while that of undergraduates and students in institutions of higher learning for adults amounted to 5,241,600. There were 9,562,700 applicants for higher education self-study examination and 542,300 who attained diplomas.

Education standards and the social value of colleges and universities have continued to improve. The educational quality of universities has advanced at a steady pace and the implementation of the "211 Project" and the "985 Project" have progressed smoothly. The cultivation of a spirit of innovation, practical thinking, and entrepreneurial passion have received greater attention. The ability of colleges and universities to solve major scientific and technological problems within the national economy and China's social development have been enhanced. The Prosperity Plan of Philosophy and Social Sciences in Colleges and Universities has been successful so far, and

THE "211 PROJECT" AND "985 PROJECT"

In July 1993, the State Education Committee issued the "Opinions on Prioritized Construction of Colleges and Universities and Key Disciplines." The committee decided to start a key project, named as "211 Project" (where "21" refers to the 21st century and "1" refers to 100 institutions of higher learning). The focus of the project was to construct around 100 higher education institutions in a selected number of key disciplines to meet the nation's needs for the 21st century. The "211 Project" was an important measure adopted by the Chinese government to advance the development of higher education and to align higher education with economic and social development.

Similarly, on May 4, 1998, at the occasion of Peking University's 100th anniversary celebratory meeting, Jiang Zemin declared that "China must have some world-class universities to be considered as a modern nation." Subsequently, the Ministry of Education shortlisted a few universities for the development of their education programs to world-class standards. This "Education Revitalization Action Program in the 21st Century" was also called the "985 Project" in short (where "98" refers to the year and "5" the month when the initiative was first declared).

has helped to promote the development and prosperity of philosophy and the social sciences in colleges and universities.

Other Areas of Reform of the Education System

The reform of educational management systems is constantly moving forward and the conditions and foundation for educational development have become more sound. The new system for managing rural compulsory education conforms to the principle of "under the leadership of the State Council, local governments take the main responsibility, manage at different levels, and focus on counties." This system has been fundamentally put in place. The new system for managing vocational education "under the leadership of the State Council,

This picture, taken on July 17, 2007, shows graduates from the School of Economics and Management, Tsinghua University at their convocation.

combining management at different levels, being based locally, government-coordinated, and featuring social participation" is essential. The higher education management system, which is "under the administration of central and provincial governments and has provincial government management as the major form" has also been further enhanced.

Recently, the reform of the school system has accelerated in tandem with private education. By 2007, there were 95,200 private schools (educational institutions, that excludes 22,300 private training institutions) of various types at different levels, with a total number of 258.35 million students.

The legislation of education has also achieved remarkable results. The Private Education Promotion Law and the Bill on Setting-up Schools Owned by Chinese-Foreign Enterprises and their enforcement regulations and policies have been promulgated. Breakthroughs were made in the amendment of the Compulsory Education Law. A number of important education laws have seen much progress in the preliminary push toward amendments and revisions while the writing of new laws and bills has also been in progress. In conclusion, the above measures have improved the national system of education laws and regulations.

Chapter 2

....

China's Science and Technology Resources and Her Talents

Current Utilization of China's Science and Technology Resources

Science and technology resources are mainly made up of science and technology manpower, governmental and non-governmental capital investments, and an implementation platform for science and technology. Since the implementation of the twin strategies to revitalize China through science and technology and her research talents, the Chinese government has been investing in the improvement of science and technology resources through its policies. It has achieved significant results in talent cultivation and utilization, the formation of a multi-technology input system under the guidance of the government, and the creation of a fundamental platform with favorable conditions for scientific research.

Overview of Science and Technology Resources

In recent years, China has witnessed a constant and rapid growth in science and technology investment, the scale of its R&D funding, the number of activities devoted to science and technology, and the number of people working in R&D. Financial and capital markets related to science and technology have also expanded, and the talent development system has been improved and fine-tuned. New progress has been made in the construction of scientific and technological competencies with a strong focus on laboratory-based research and independent innovation, supported by a public service platform. All these provide favorable conditions for the development of scientific and technological research and the commercialization of a large number of research results.

According to official statistics, expenditure on R&D in 2007 totaled RMB 371.02 billion, 26.1 times the amount spent in 1991 and with an annual increase of 22.6%. In 2007, the proportion of R&D expenditure in GDP was 1.49%, with an increase of 0.84 base points compared with 1991. This shows that the allocation of social resources to independent R&D has increased on an annual basis.

In 2006, China's R&D investment ranked sixth in the world behind the United States, Japan, Germany, France, and the United Kingdom. In terms of the sources for science and technology funds, 67.44% came from private enterprises, 22.14% from the government, and 4.99% from financial institutions. In terms of R&D investment, the proportion of R&D invested by enterprises continued to grow, and accounted for 72.28% in 2007. The ratio of fundamental research to applied research to laboratory-based research was 1:2.8:17.4 in 2007.

Since the start of reform and opening up in 1978, China's science and technology manpower have undergone rapid recovery and development. By the

China's science and technology resources (2003–2007)

Indicators	2003	2004	2005	2006	2007
Staff in science and technology activities					
(10,000)	328.4	348.1	381.5	413.2	454.4
• Scientists and engineers	225.5	225.2	256.1	279.8	312.9
Funds raised for science and technology					
(RMB 100 million)	3,459.1	4,328.3	5,250.8	6,196.7	7,695.2
• Government funds	3,459.1	4,328.3	5,250.8	6,196.7	7,659.2
• Enterprise funds	2,053.3	2,771.2	3,440.3	4,106.9	5,189.5
• Loans by financial institutions	259.3	265.0	276.8	374.3	384.3
Expenditure on R&D (RMB 100 million)	1,539.6	1,966.3	2,450.0	3,003.1	3,710.2
• Basic research	87.7	117.2	131.2	155.8	174.5
• Applied research	311.4	400.5	433.5	489.0	492.9
• Laboratory-based research	1,140.5	1,448.7	1,885.3	2,358.4	3,042.8
Proportion of R&D expenditure in GDP (%)	1.13	1.23	1.34	1.42	1.49

Source: *China Statistical Yearbook (2008)*

end of 2007, there were 225.5 million technicians, 5.2 times the figure for 1978. The technicians can be categorized into five specific types, such as engineering and technical personnel; agricultural technicians; scientific research personnel; health technicians; and teaching staff.

While these personnel continue to increase in numbers, the skill and quality of these science and technology R&D personnel are also improving. This has resulted in a large pool of highly qualified science and technology manpower. At present, the number of R&D personnel in China is second in the world after the United States.

Allocation of Science and Technology Resources

The allocation and funding of financial resources for science and technology from the central government, local governments, private enterprises, and financial institutions is described here. After that, the policies implemented in training of human resources for science and technology is discussed briefly.

Funding from the Central Government   Direct funding by the central government originates mainly from the state budget, which can be divided into direct financing and equity financing. Direct financing includes a budget allocated by the central government while equity financing refers to financing through various equity methods. From 2001 to 2006, science and technology funding from the state budget continued to increase. By 2006, the amount reached RMB 100.97 billion, 2.27 times the figure for 2001. Besides arranging such funding, the state budget also allocates a separate sum for other projects not included in the above science and technology expenditures.

Indirect funding comes from preferential tax breaks or tax holidays and are an important part of science and technology funding from the central government. Based on the implementation of preferential tax policies on science and technology, a series of specific tax measures were issued in 2007. In the new enterprise income tax law and related enforcement regulations, it is prescribed that high-tech enterprises can enjoy a low tax rate of 15% and major adjustments on the taxable amounts were also decided.

Funding from Local Governments   Science and technology funding by local governments can also be broken down into direct and indirect funding. Direct funding refers to financial capital investment that local governments make through equity investment. Indirect funding refers to capital investments generated by the implementation of a preferential tax policy.

In 2007, local expenditures on science and technology amounted to RMB 85.844 billion. Science and technology spending in Shanghai and Guangdong both exceeded RMB 10 billion. Expenditures on science and technology by local funding took up 2.24% of local fiscal expenditures in 2007. A total of nine provinces exceeded 2%, while Guangdong, Zhejiang, and Shanghai exceeded 3%, with Beijing having the highest rate of 5.5%. Meanwhile, local governments at all levels thoroughly implemented science and technology preferential tax policies based on their local conditions.

Funding from Private Enterprises In recent years, private enterprises have become a major force in supporting the rapid increase in science and technology investment. In 2007, funds raised for scientific and technological activities by private enterprises reached RMB 518.948 billion, an phenomenal increase of 26.4% as compared to 2006.

The R&D funding intensity of private enterprises is an important indicator for measuring the ability of private enterprises to develop technology. Between 1991 and 1998, the R&D funding intensity of large and medium-sized industrial enterprises stayed constant at a level of 0.5%. Starting from 1999, the R&D funding intensity of private enterprises began to climb upward, reaching 0.76% in 2006 and 0.81% in 1997.

This picture shows the headquarters of the China Development Bank in Beijing. The bank is a policy-oriented financial institution directly managed by the State Council that provides loans to high-tech enterprises.

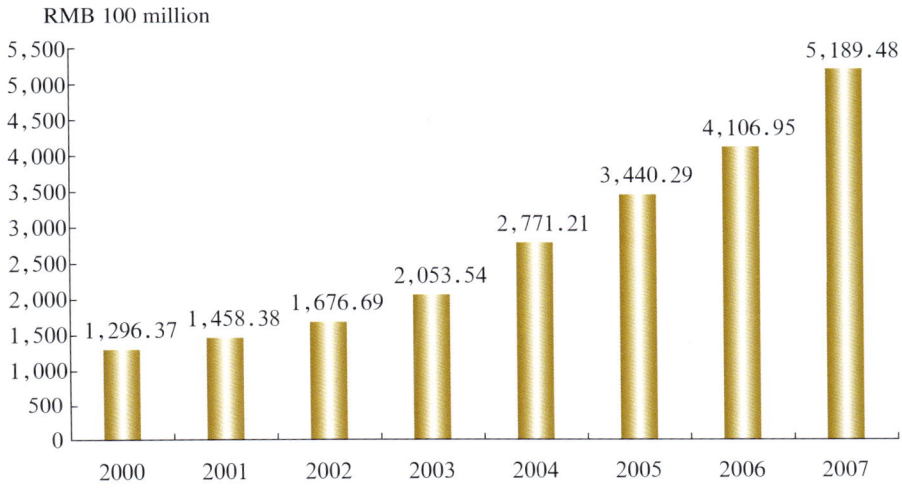

Source: *Statistical Yearbook of China Science and Technology (2008)*

Science and technology funding from private enterprises (2000–2007)

Funding from Financial Institutions The number of venture capital institutions in 2007 totaled 383, among which 69 were newly established. The amount of venture capital reached RMB 111.29 billion, with RMB 44.92 billion being allocated to new investments. As for the capital market, 237 companies were listed on the Small and Medium Enterprise Board of the

TD-SCDMA

TD-SCDMA is an international 3G communications standard with independent property rights and was proposed by Datang Mobile. Compared to W-CDMA of Europe and CDMA2000 of the United States, TD-SCDMA has unique technical advantages. Recommended by the Ministry of Science and Technology, the National Development Bank granted RMB 200 million through a technical assistance loan to the TD-SCDMA project in June 2004. This was a groundbreaking event as it was the first attempt by the National Development Bank to support key national science and technology projects through intellectual property mortgages which provided an example of cooperation between science and technology and public finance.

Shenzhen Stock Exchange in 2007. The average income from their principal business reached RMB 1.131 billion, an increase of 30.12% over the same period for the previous year. According to official statistics, a total of 27 companies listed on all three boards[1] in China had an income of RMB 3.38 billion from their principal business in 2007, an increase of 40.4% over the previous year.

Nurturing Talents in Science and Technology   Talents in science and technology refer to human resources that are actually engaged in or have the potential to work on the systematic production and application of scientific and technological knowledge. To implement the strategy of revitalizing the country through talents in the new century, government departments have successively introduced or continued to strengthen policies to develop human resources in science and technology and have worked out a series of programs to cultivate talent.

The "Million Talents in the New Century" is a special project started to cultivate professional and technical personnel. It is organized and implemented by the Ministry of Personnel, the Ministry of Science and Technology, the Ministry of Finance, the National Development and Reform Commission,

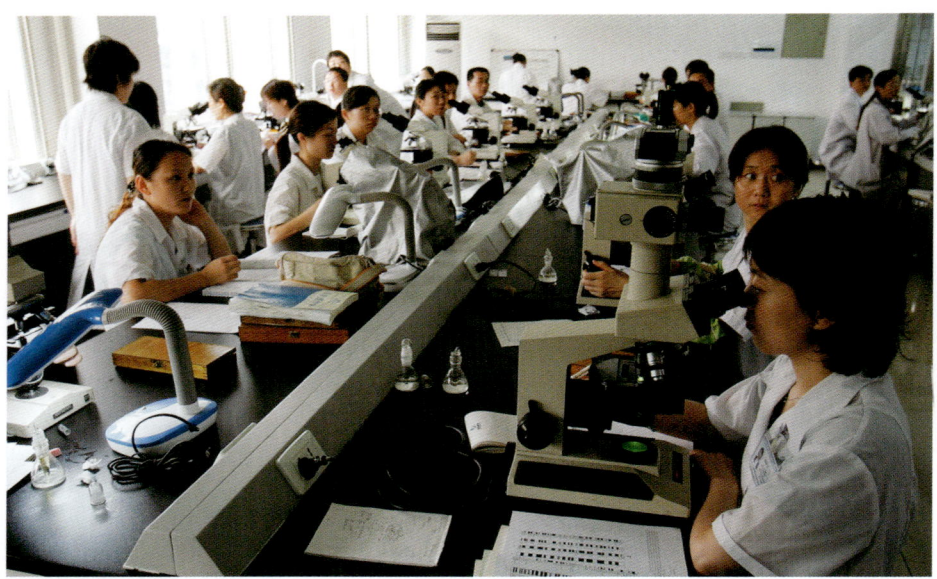

This picture shows medical researchers working in the State Key Laboratory of Medical Genetics of Central South University in Changsha City, Hunan.

---

[1] The stock exchanges of Shanghai, Hong Kong, and Shenzhen.

the National Natural Science Foundation, and the China Association for Science. In 2006, the project selected 3,841 experts to receive special government allowances. Another 530 young and middle-aged high-potential technical professionals were selected as state-level candidates.

The implementation of major national science and technology programs such as the "863 Program,"[2] the National Key Science and Technology R&D

YUAN LONGPING, THE FATHER OF HYBRID RICE

Yuan Longping was born in 1930. He is an expert on the research of Chinese paddy hybrids and an academician of the Chinese Academy of Engineering. Currently, he is the Director-General of the China National Hybrid Rice Research and Development Center and the principal consultant for the UN Food and Agriculture Organization. He was elected a foreign academician at the U.S. National Academy of Sciences in April 2006. He is known as the "Father of Hybrid Rice" worldwide.

Yuan Longping is the first scientist to successfully apply hybrid rice heterosis (also known as outbreeding enhancement) in commercial production around the world. He successfully bred general hybrid rice and achieved success in developing Super Hybrid Rice 1, 2, and 3, improving the average yield per mu ($\approx$0.0667 hectares) of Chinese rice from 300 kg to 500 kg, and then subsequently pushing it to 700 kg before reaching 800 kg!

From 1976 to 2006, China has dedicated 370 million hectares to hybrid rice cultivation. The increase in rice production each year can feed 70 million people. Meanwhile, hybrid rice has spread to more than 30 countries and regions around the world.

Yuan Longping has trained a large number of hybrid rice experts and technicians. He has conducted over 20 international training courses on hybrid rice, training more than 500 technicians in over 30 countries. He has built and improved a set of theoretical and applied technology systems during his research and development of hybrid rice, creating a new discipline in the study of hybrid rice.

---

[2] The "86" refers to the year 1986 and "3" the month of March when the program was created. It was also endorsed by Deng Xiaoping.

This picture shows Yuan Longping examining the growth of some hybrid rice.

Program and the "973 Program"[3] have set the stage for young scientists and technicians to display their talents. These programs have become a cradle to cultivate young leaders and talents of high caliber, such as doctorate and masters students. By 2007, the three major science and technology programs had produced 9,822 PhD holders and 16,532 masters graduates.

China's postdoctoral system has attracted and retained a large number of high-level experts, resulting in the emergence of a highly qualified postdoctoral research team. Their research subjects cover 86 important areas in 12 disciplines, including science, industry, agriculture, medicine, philosophy, and social sciences. They also covered important fields closely related to the national economy and people's livelihood such as industries, agriculture, national defense, transportation, energy, and environmental protection.

The "100 Talents Program" is an important talent program implemented by the Chinese Academy of Sciences. The program plans to attract 100 Chinese talents from abroad and 30 from within China. By end-2007, the Chinese Academy of Sciences had introduced and cultivated 1,417 high-level science

---

[3] The program was finalized and implemented on June 4, 1997. It is also known as the National Basic Research Program. More details available here: http://www.973.gov.cn/English/Index.aspx.

WANG XUAN—FOUNDER OF THE COMPUTERIZED CHINESE CHARACTERS LASER TYPESETTING SYSTEM

Wang Xuan (1937–2006) was a professor at Peking University and was the founder and technical director of the computerized Chinese Characters Laser Typesetting System. The system was developed by his research group and laid the foundation for the computerized typesetting of newspapers and print publications. The system is hailed as the "second invention of Chinese printing."

Wang Xuan's work was well received by the market and he was praised as a market-oriented scientist. From 1981, he focused on the commercialization of his research and built a computerized Chinese characters laser typesetting system in 1985. This brought about enormous economic and social benefits. After 1988, as the main founder and Chief Technology Advisor of the Founder Group (created and set-up by Peking University), he actively advocated market-oriented technology research and created a successful method for integrating industrial manufacturing and research.

and technology manpower and 178 winners of the China National Funds for Distinguished Young Scientists, who were awarded dedicated grants from the program.

The current number and variety of science and technology manpower demonstrates the growth of science and technology. The proportion of high-level talent among science and technology manpower continues to rise. The distribution of personnel in scientific and technological activities and R&D personnel in private enterprises, research institutes, and institutions of higher learning has become more reasonable. Young and middle-aged personnel have become the most significant group of science and technology manpower.

Sharing of Science and Technology Resources

To date, the push to establish an information platform for important science and technology resources has helped change the former situation of scattered, redundant, and inefficient allocation of science and technology resources. The

This picture, taken on September 27, 2005, shows Professor Wang Xuan holding an academic discussion with his foreign counterparts during the *Fortune* magazine's Technology Roundtable.

platform has also improved the efficiency of science and technology investments from the central government. It has revitalized a substantial number of national science and technology resources.

Shared Platform for Large-scale Scientific Instruments and Equipment A sharing platform for large scientific instruments and equipment includes the construction and reorganization of resources of large scientific instruments and equipment, the construction and improvement of the National Center for Large-Scale Scientific Instruments, Analysis, and Testing, the construction of the National Testing Resources Sharing Platform, and the construction of the Resource-Sharing Platform for the National Measurement Base Standard System. By October 2007, the National Large-Scale Instrument Coordination and Sharing Network had collected and reorganized 14,770 information resources on instruments and equipment that cost over RMB 400,000. Through various distinctive services outside the network, the efficiency in the use of instruments has been by and large improved.

Shared Resource Platform for Natural Sciences and Technology The shared resources platform for the natural sciences and technology includes the creation of eight resource areas such as plant germplasm; animal germplasm; microbial, rock, and mineral fossil specimens; reference materials; human genetic resources; biological specimens; and experimental materials.

From this resources platform, an integrated *e*-platform of national natural sciences and technology resources is now accessible throughout the country. This platform includes 32 portals that cover eight areas of the natural sciences and technology and a shared information network made up of 535 databases related to natural sciences and technology. These resources provide an important support to major national scientific research. For example, it is now possible to effectively reserve and share experimental and reference materials. At the end of 2006, the shared platform for natural sciences and technology resources had supplied 448,000 different resources to scientific research projects. The frequency of resource sharing grew to three times as compared to the period before the establishment of the platform.

Shared Platform for Scientific Data Through years of accumulation, the variety and amount of data available at 12 scientific data sharing centers (or networks) grew rapidly. The data include research areas such as meteorology, earthquakes, cartography, forestry and agriculture, oceanography, land resources, and industrial engineering. Through reorganization and sharing, these data resources were developed with government investments and a net worth of more than RMB 25 billion were revitalized.

This data platform updated and enlarged a large number of databases with total data storage in excess of 3,160 gigabytes. It also saved, reserved, and carried out digital processing on a large quantity of important scientific historical data that would otherwise be lost. It also provided basic data support to major programs such as the "973 Program," the "863 Program," the National Key Technology R&D Program, and the National Natural Science Foundation.

Shared Platform for Scientific and Technological Publications The establishment of the National Science and Technology Library (NSTL) marked the mutual creation and sharing of cross-departmental and cross-system resources and services in science, engineering, agriculture, and medicine. This library propels the progress of information services in local areas and departments by building a distribution system and implementing preferential policies in the western regions of China. In 2007, the network received 123,953 requests for information services, amounting to 81% of the total annual information requests for that year.

The Standard Publications Shared Services Network technically makes it possible to organize resources, share information, and coordinate services within the country. By prescribing 10 standard data processing specifications, which include standard recording specifications, standard classifications, and quality control specifications on domestic and foreign standard publications, among others, the network reorganizes more than 400,000 pieces of national, industrial, and local standard resources. It also provides users with standard information services through the China Standard Service Network.

Science and Technology Network Progress has been made in the application system of the National Sci-Tech Basic Condition Platform, which is stil under construction. The platform involves the building of a network for high-performance scientific computing environments, a network-based coordinating environment, a testing environment, and standard specifications for the platform. Through the construction of a network-based coordinating environment, China has realized the remote control of some large-scale instruments. The world's first "micro-beam large-scale scientific instrument virtual networked laboratory" project has also been implemented in the public service system. The social benefits of the China Digital Science and Technology Museum have gradually becoming evident.

CHINA DIGITAL SCIENCE AND TECHNOLOGY MUSEUM

The China Digital Science and Technology Museum (www.cdstm.cn) is an Internet-based national public science service platform built by the China Association for Science, the Ministry of Education, and the Chinese Academy of Sciences. The task of the China Digital Science and Technology Museum is to stimulate the public's (and especially the younger population's) interest in science and enhance the quality of scientific information available to the public. It also aims to build a network for those with scientific interest. On the China Digital Science and Technology Museum, the public can acquire scientific knowledge, experience scientific processes, stimulate innovation, scan science and technology news, and share rich scientific resources.

By the end of 2007, the China Digital Science and Technology Museum had mostly completed the construction of the exhibition hall (Hall A) with eight virtual museums and six network science columns, the Experience Hall (Hall B), and the science resources section, covering nine areas in the Resource Hall (Hall C). In November 2007, the museum won an award in the *e*-science category in the 2007 World Information Summit initiated by the United Nations and the World Summit on Information Society.

Transfer of Scientific and Technological Achievements to the Public Service Platform   The Public Service Platform was built in 2005 to provide a reliable service to scientific research personnel and to assist economic development throughout the country. In February 2007, the platform completed the development of its information and service portal system on national scientific and technological achievements.

Apart from the construction of the National Science and Technology Basic Specifications Platform, all the different regions in China developed their unique platforms based on the local resource advantages and local needs for industrial development. They focused on the transformation of scientific and technological achievements as well as providing public technical services to small and medium-sized enterprises. All these initiatives are useful explorations on the mechanism and mode for local and regional platform construction.

FYI
FOR YOUR INFORMATION

THE SHANGHAI R&D PUBLIC SERVICE PLATFORM

The Shanghai R&D Public Service Platform (www.sgst.cn) was founded in 2004. The R&D platform is an open scientific and technological infrastructure and public service system built through the use of modern technologies such as information technology and networks. It consists of ten systems—scientific data sharing, scientific and technological literature services, equipment facility sharing, resource conditions protection, testing base collaboration, professional technology services, industry testing services, business incubation services, and management decision support.

As an important part of the National Science and Technology Basic Conditions Platform, the Shanghai R&D Public Service Platform will effectively integrate the R&D resources of the Shanghai and Yangtze River Delta region and promote an efficient allocation and sharing of science and technology resources for the general public. It will also enhance the independent innovation capacity of enterprises and lower innovation and start-up costs. In addition, the platform will strengthen co-operation between production and research, systematically optimize the environment for scientific and technological innovation and industrialization, and provide a strong support for the comprehensive upgrading of Shanghai's international competitiveness in science and technology.

Science and Technology Talents

Education and Talent Resources

The rapid development of China's higher education has enhanced the supply of trained science and technology personnel. Institutions of higher learning have cultivated a large number of high-quality talent for China. The gross enrollment rate has jumped from 12.5% in 2000 to 23.0% in 2007. Before the expansion of college enrollments in 1998, the number of college students in institutions of higher learning was only 64.3 million. Since then, it has increased to 271.95 million (excluding the group of self-study students who were taking the courses) by the end of 2007.

Graduates are the major source of science and technology personnel. In 2007, there were 7.27 million undergraduates from regular colleges and universities, institutions of higher learning for adults, and cyber colleges for online learning. Of these, university graduates accounted for 3.15 million, while 4.12 million were graduates from professional training colleges. The number of postgraduates was 311,800, of which 41,500 held doctorates and 270,300 masters degrees.

Natural sciences and engineering graduates are the primary sources of scientists and engineers. Starting from the year 2000, the number of graduates majoring in natural sciences and engineering has increased significantly, providing a large number of young scientists and technicians to all sectors of the national economy.

STATUS OF CHINA'S HIGHER EDUCATION GRADUATES IN 2007

In 2007, the number of graduates who majored in natural sciences and engineering from universities and professional training colleges totaled 22.14 million. Among these, graduates who majored in engineering accounted for the largest number of of 15.94 million. Medicine graduates came in second, numbering 300,000. Science and agriculture majors make up 231,000 and 88,000, respectively.

In 2007, the number of postgraduates in the natural sciences and engineering reached 193,600. Of these, 30,300 earned doctorates and the remaining 163,300 gained masters degrees. Among postgraduates, students majoring in science took up 11.3%, those in engineering accounted for 36.8%, and those in agriculture and medicine accounted for 3.6% and 10.4%, respectively.

In 2007, a total of 88,059 people participated in projects organized by the National Natural Science Foundation of China, as well as those held by the Youth Science Foundation and local science funds. There were 11,608 project leaders linked to the National Natural Science Foundation, Youth Science Foundation, and local science funds. Some 6,011 research personnel obtained funding support for key science projects. The National Outstanding Youth Science Foundation sponsored 170 domestic and 10 foreign young scholars. Overseas, Hong Kong, and Macau Joint Research Funds for Young Scholars provided funds for 80 foreign young scholars. The National Training Fund for Basic Sciences sponsored 60 hubs for national basic science training and teaching research, and funding for 72 projects. The Innovative Scientific Research Group Fund offered support to 29 innovation research groups and additional funds to another 24 research groups.

Status of Investment in Talent Development

During the 10th Five-Year Plan period, China vigorously developed her education and strengthened the training of her science and technology personnel. Consequently, China saw a rapid increase and constant optimization in the total number and structure of science and technology manpower. The country also made significant progress in the training of personnel and attracting overseas science and technology manpower to serve the nation.

Status of Local Investment in Science and Technology Manpower In recent years, investment in science and technology manpower in eastern, central, and western China has seen an overall increase. From 2000 to 2006, the total number of R&D manpower and R&D scientists and engineers in the eastern areas maintained an annual growth rate of 10.9% and 11.8%, respectively. The rates in central China were 7.3% and 9.1%, respectively. However, the same indicators in the western part of China were only 2.9% and 5.0%, respectively.

The development of science and technology manpower in central and western China has shown significant improvements in recent years. Out of the past six years, there were low increases and even negative growth for three years. Although the increases in 2005 and 2006 were rapid, the gap between eastern China and the rest of the country continues to widen. Between 2000 and 2006, the proportion of R&D manpower and R&D scientists and engineers in eastern China compared to the national total increased from 54.0% and 55.7% to 61.2% and 61.4%, respectively. The same indicators in central China, however, experienced a decrease of 23.4% and 22.9% to 21.8% and 21.9%, respectively. For the western part of China, the indicators dropped from 22.6% and 21.4% to 17.0% and 16.7%, respectively. The science and technology talents of China continue to show a tendency toward a concentration in her eastern areas.

Manpower Projects by the Ministry of Education Based on the overall planning, integration, and organization, as well as inheritance and innovation from the ongoing 10 talent projects, the Ministry of Education launched the "High-level Innovative Talent Plan" in 2004. The first level refers to the "Cheung Kong Scholars Program" and the "Innovative Team Development Program." The former program selects and appoints 100 Cheung Kong Scholars, who are distinguished visiting professors, and another 100 scholars. The latter program selects and sponsors 60 innovative teams. The second level refers to the "New Century Excellent Talent Support Program," which selects and funds 1,000 outstanding young academic leaders in the natural sciences, humanities, and the social sciences. The third level is the "Young Core Teacher Training Program," which provides key support to over 10,000 young teachers.

From 1998 to 2006, a total of 97 institutions of higher learning employed 799 distinguished visiting professors, and 308 professors. Fourteen outstanding scholars also won the Cheung Kong Scholars Achievement Award.

The Postgraduate Education Innovation Program is an important part of the Ministry of Education's 2003–2007 Action Plan for Invigorating Education

This picture, taken on March 28, 2005, shows the Conferment Ceremony of the 2004 Cheung Kong Scholars and Visiting Professors held at the Great Hall of the People in Beijing. The Cheung Kong Scholars Program was launched in August 1998. It has become a status icon for China's high-level manpower in science and technology and has produced much scientific research and education innovation among institutions of higher learning.

that was approved by the State Council. This program includes a series of action programs to create the National Academic Forum, the National Graduate Summer School, the National Doctoral Academic Conferences, the Graduate Innovation Center, the Visiting Postgraduate System, and the Graduate Education Reform.

In 2006, the Ministry of Education carried out 85 graduate education innovation programs. Among these, there were 13 National Doctoral Academic Forums held in various sub-disciplines and 14 National Graduate Summer Schools. In addition, the Postgraduate Education Innovation Program enlarged its support for visiting fellows, providing funds to 25 graduate education units to receive visting graduates from other universities in their key disciplines and key laboratories.

Attraction of Science and Technology Manpower The Chinese government has adopted an open policy for talent cultivation and overseas studies, allowing her citizens to study abroad, attract foreign students to study in China. It has even attracted overseas talents to work in China by offering preferential policies and measures. This policy has accelerated the domestic and foreign flow of science and technology manpower. The flow is not only conducive to the cultivation and development of science and technology manpower, but also promotes the spread and utilization of scientific and technological knowledge.

In recent years, a great number of Chinese citizens were studying abroad, and the number of such citizens returning to China has grown every year. Statistics issued by UNESCO show that China now has the largest number of students studying abroad, with one Chinese student for every seven foreign students around the world. Since 2000, the number of Chinese citizens returning to China has grown. In 2007, the number of Chinse citizens studying abroad reached 144,000, while the number returning totaled 44,000. Out of the number of Chinese citizens studying abroad, 30.6% of them returned to China after their studies.

This picture, taken on September 24, 2008, shows the opening ceremony of the China Overseas Students Liaoning Entrepreneurship Week, held in Dalian City. The entrepreneurship week provided multiple platforms and sessions for the exchange of information on new businesses, talents, capital, and financing. This created a bridge to help returning students to start businesses and look for jobs.

With the growing influence of China's economy around the world, Chinese colleges and universities have become highly attractive to young foreign students. In recent years, the number of foreign students has increased by more than 20% every year. In 2005, the number of foreign students in China topped 140,000. To encourage Chinese citizens who study abroad to return to work in China or serve the country through various channels, the Chinese government adopted a series of policies and measures.

The Ministry of Education successively established programs such as the Returned Overseas Students Scientific Research Initiative Fund, the Beyond the 21st Century Talents Program, and the Spring Sunshine Program. In 2005, to improve the effectiveness of programs for attracting overseas Chinese students, the Ministry of Personnel, the Ministry of Education, the Ministry of Science and Technology, and the Ministry of Finance jointly issued the Opinions on Defining High-level Returned Overseas Talents in the Introduction of Overseas Talents.

In 2006, the Ministry of Personnel formulated and published the Plan for Students Returning to Work in the 11th Five-Year Plan. During the 11th Five-Year Plan period (2006–2010), China carried out three major programs to attract overseas Chinese talents to serve the country: the Concentration of High-level Overseas Talents Plan, the Overseas Talents Business Plan, and the Plan to Serve the Country through Wisdom. In order to implement these plans, a policy and coordinating department was set up to attract overseas Chinese students to return to work and serve the country. In addition, a green channel for high-level overseas Chinese talents to return to work has been provided.

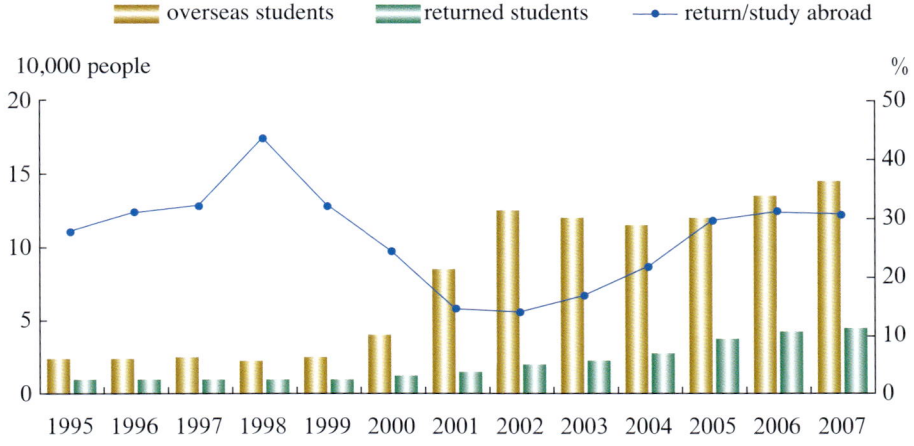

Source: *China Statistical Yearbook (2008)*

Overseas Students and Returned Students (1995–2007)

THREE KINDS OF TALENTS

China wishes to attract three types of talents: academic and technology leaders, senior management personnel, and other experts that are lacking in the country. Through the leadership of national key laboratories, academic leaders of institutions of higher learning, scientific research institutes, and other senior research personnel, China conducted recruitment road-shows overseas and concentrated on attracting a number of science and technology leaders and senior scientists researching strategic disciplines.

Combined with major national science and technology projects and key innovation projects, China has actively introduced high-level foreign talents and research groups, integrating the independent innovation strategy and concentrating on key national development areas such as energy, water, and mineral resources; the environment and agriculture; and cutting-edge technologies in biotechnology, new materials, and advanced manufacturing. China mainly targets overseas Chinese talents that hold independent and innovative intellectual property rights and patents and possesses high potential to contribute to national development.

These projects aim to increase the number of newly returned overseas Chinese talents to reach 150,000 to 200,000, to attract 200,000 overseas Chinese students to return to work in China, to build 150 pioneer parks for overseas Chinese talents, and to ensure that the number of enterprises introducing overseas Chinese talents reaches 10,000.

The National University Science Park and the Overseas Students Pioneer Park promoted by the Chinese government provide favorable conditions for overseas students to return home and set up businesses. To do this, the government offers a series of policies to encourage overseas students to return. One of these policies include government support for overseas talents to commercially exploit their patents, proprietary technology, and scientific research results to run enterprises. Furthermore, the government provides preferential conditions to enterprises established by overseas talents with regard to taxation, financing, and manpower recruitment.

These policies also cover the following areas:

- the setting up and improvement of investment and financing mechanisms required for running either business or high-tech enterprises;
- the establishment of national enterprise funds for overseas talents; and
- the encouragement and support of pioneer parks with capabilities to attract and set up venture capital funds and pioneering funds and that provides access to capital and financing guarantees for returning overseas talents.

By 2006, there were 50 university science parks approved by the Ministry of Science and Technology and 6,075 enterprises had established offices in these parks. Out of this number, 1,746 were high-tech enterprises and 1,110 were business enterprises founded by teachers and students from institutions of higher learning. There were 21 pilot units for the national overseas talents pioneering park approved by the Ministry of Personnel, the Ministry of Science and Technology, the Ministry of Education, and the State Association of Industry and Commerce. Throughout the country, there are 110 overseas talent pioneer parks at various levels. More than 6,000 enterprises have moved into these parks and around 15,000 overseas talents run their businesses there.

The policies and measures China has adopted to attract overseas Chinese talents have generated good results. Many overseas Chinese talents have joined research institutes and institutions of higher learning, and have participated in national science and technology R&D projects and other scientific research and teaching activities. In 2006, three major science and technology plans—the 863 Program, National Key Technology R&D Program, and the 973 Program attracted 2,734 talents, of whom 2,388 were overseas Chinese students and the remaining 346 were foreign experts.

In 2006, the number of PhDs returning from overseas study and working in Chinese research institutes reached 1,787, accounting for 9.6% of the total number of PhDs in research institutes. The number of returned PhDs with leadership positions hit 226, taking up 12.6% of the total number of returned PhDs working at research institutes. Among universities and colleges directly under the Ministry of Education, 72% of presidents had gained experience studying abroad as had 63% of PhD supervisors and 72% of directors in teaching and research centers and key laboratories at the state or provincial level. A total of 81% of academicians at the Chinese Academy of Sciences, 54% of academicians at the Chinese Academy of Engineering, and 72% of chief scientists in the 863 Program are all talents who returned from overseas studies.

This picture shows the Tsinghua Science Park, that is based in Beijing Zhongguancun Science Park. Since its establishment in 1994, it has become one of the fastest growing zones with a high occupancy rate and high quality enterprises. It is the only Class A university park for science and technology in the country.

Chapter 3

China's Scientific and Technological Progress and Innovations

The implementation of a series of national science and technology projects and programs has effectively promoted the scientific and technological development of China. This has improved the independent innovation capacity in scientific and high-tech research. Laws and regulations that secure scientific and technological progress, innovation, and system reform have further improved the construction of a national innovation system.

National Science and Technology Planning and Implementation

National Science and Technology Planning

The prescription of mid- and long-term science and technology planning is conducive to the organization of long-term scientific and technological work. For instance, it can provide overall design and instruction for the building of basic scientific and technological capacities and disciplinary adjustments, which require long-term and stable support. Since 1949, the Chinese government has developed seven science and technology plans. Beside these, the government has drawn up special science and technology development plans based on scientific and technological development needs. China has used the primary strategy of combining long-term development plans for science and technology with mid- to short-term science and technology plans to allocate science and technology resources and the organization of scientific activities.

The 1956–1967 Science and Technology Development Outline Plan was the first long-term plan for scientific and technological development of China. Proposed in the plan were 57 major scientific and technological tasks in 13 areas, 616 central problems that were further integrated, and another 12 key tasks. The plan also laid down general prescriptions for a national scientific research system, existing manpower utilization principles, general planning for training and the allocation of leaders, and principles for establishing scientific research institutes. It was a plan that focused on the arrangements of projects, talents, centers of research, and mechanisms and policies. The implementation of the plan played a decisive role in the setup of China's scientific research institutes, the adjustment of disciplines, and major research areas in institutions of higher learning, the formulation and development of scientific and technological teams, the system and methods of science and technology management, and the shaping of the overall science and technology system.

In the following decades, the Chinese government drew up the 1963–1972 Outline for the Science and Technology Plan, the 1978–1985 National Science and Technology Development Plan, the 1986–2000 Science and Technology Development Plan, and time-limited, mid- to long-term science

FYI
FOR YOUR INFORMATION
THE FIVE-YEAR PLAN

The Five-Year Plan is part of China's national economic plan, its main function is to develop plans for major national construction projects, distribute the labor force accordingly, provide forecasts for key national economic ratios, and lay down objectives and orientation for long-term national economic development. Except for the period between 1949 and 1952, which was a period of national economic recovery, and between 1963 and 1965, a period of national economic adjustment, China has implemented 11 Five-Year Plans. The first was in 1953. To adapt to the new development of a socialist market economy, the Chinese government will switch her focus from planning into regulation, starting from the 11th Five-Year Plan period (2006–2010).

In 1965, Chinese biologists were the first to successfully produce synthetic bovine insulin. Bovine insulin was the first synthetic protein, marking a huge step in the scientific understanding of life.

and technology development plans that include the Ten-Year Plan for Science and Technology Development for 1991–2000, the Eighth Five-Year Plan (1991–1995), the National Science and Technology Development Ninth Five-Year Plan (1996–2000), the 2010 Long-term Development Plan, and the Special Plan on Science and Technology Development of the 10th Five-Year Plan for the National Economy and Social Development.

In 2004, the Chinese government began to draft the first outline of the National Mid- to Long-term Science and Technology Development Plan (2006–2020) for the 21st century.

On February 9, 2006, the State Council released the National Mid- to Long-Term Science and Technology Development Plan (2006–2020), and selected 68 priority subjects with clearly defined missions and possible breakthroughs out of the key fields for the national economy and social development, which require urgent scientific and technological support.

National Science and Technology Programs

To implement the tasks and objectives of the National Mid- to Long-term Science and Technology Development Plan, the government has worked out special science and technology development plans for specific key areas on science and technology that bear considerable significance to the national economy and national security. During the 11th Five-Year Plan period, the

This picture, taken on January 9, 2009, shows the 2008 National Science and Technology Award Conference held in the Great Hall of the People in Beijing.

national science and technology plans centered on the national economic and social development objectives specified in the plan, and provided strong support for the removal of bottlenecks in the process of economic and social development, the advance of industrial competitiveness, the safeguard of national security, and the construction of a harmonious society.

General Framework During the 11th Five-Year Plan period, various national science and technology plans built up its planning system by strengthening macro control, improving levels of management, and improving efficiency. The system conforms to the socialist market economic system and the requirements of scientific and technological development. Simply, it is "specific in rights and responsibilities, clear in position, reasonable in structure, and efficient in operation." It has changed the former "3+2" planning system into one that consists of major projects and basic plans.

Major projects include strategic product development, key common technology research, and major construction projects supported, organized, and carried out by the government. Such measures reflect the strategic objectives of the nation.

The basic plans consist of master plans and policy-guiding plans. Master plans cover the National Basic Research Program, the National Key Technology R&D Program, the National High-tech R&D Program, and the Construction of the National Science and Technology Basic Condition Platform. Government-guided plans mainly include the Spark Plan, the Torch Plan, technological innovation-guided projects, and the New Products Program.

New Position Adopted by the National Science and Technology Plan   To fully implement the development tasks of major projects, key areas, and their priority subjects, the government has used advanced technologies, basic research, and the construction of scientific and technological basic conditions written in the Out-line of the National Mid- to Long-Term Science and Technology Development Plan. Similarly, the government is repositioning all science and technology plans in the 11th Five-Year Plan period. The major tasks are as follows:

Implementation of the rapid development of major projects. The 11th Five-Year Plan focused on the organization and implementation of major projects that are urgently required in the national economy and social development. On this basis, the government worked out the overall major key technologies that could propel development, produce a number of world-class advanced major strategic products and technical systems, and cultivate strategic industries and internation-ally competitive businesses. Other key commitments included the construction of a few landmark projects to improve the international standing of China and

SPARK PROGRAM

The Spark Program, initiated in early 1986, was the first instructive science and technology plan approved by the Chinese government to promote rural economic development through scientific and technological progress. In May 1985, the National Science Commission proposed a plan to the State Council for focusing on a number of short-term, stable, and rapidly developed science and technology programs to propel local economic revitalization. In this plan, a Chinese proverb was cited: "A single spark can start a prairie fire." The program was thus named the Spark Program, implying that the spark of science and technology would spread through the vast rural areas of China.

enhance national pride, increasing efforts to achieve breakthroughs in certain key research areas to realize development in scientific and technological innovation.

Implementation of science and technology support plans, solving of outstanding problems, and breakthroughs in development bottlenecks. Based on the existing national science and technology research plans, support for the R&D of major public technologies was further strengthened, and outstanding issues that required urgent settlement in national economic and social development were clearly defined. Combined with major construction projects and the development of major equipments, the focus is on solving the major cross-sector and cross-regional technical problems, overcoming problems in key technologies, as well as eliminating constraints to enhance industrial competitiveness and promote harmonious social development. At the same time, in order to enhance the scientific and technological support capacity and independent innovation ability of industries, national authorities carried out futuristic, contingent, and fundamental research in the sectors of agriculture, forestry, irrigation, meteorology, earthquake, disaster relief, quality inspection, environmental protection, traditional Chinese medicine, and sanitation during the 11th Five-Year Plan period.

Implementation of high-tech R&D plans, achievement of breakthroughs in cutting-edge technologies, and for future development. During the 11th Five-Year Plan period, the National High-tech R&D Plan (or the 863 Plan) centered on the requirements of developing cutting-edge technologies, transforming the center from following new development to its advanced deployment. The plan focused on leading future development and constructing an overall organization for the research, development, and integrated application of cutting-edge technologies by following strategies and realizing visions. Research in main cutting-edge technologies to achieve breakthroughs was further strengthened. The plans also cultivated new industrial growth points and led the development of high-tech industries and emerging industries by strengthening the integration of and innovation in cutting-edge technologies.

Implementation of the National Natural Science Foundation Program and the National Major Basic R&D Plan to enhance original innovation. The National Natural Science Foundation Program focused on free explorative fundamental research and tackles development in basic disciplines, inter-disciplines, and emerging disciplines, as well as eight frontier scientific problems detailed in the Outline for the National Mid- to Long-term Science and Technology Development Plan. The National Major Basic R&D Plan (or the 973 Program) centered on national goals and research, organizes, and carries out fundamental research that is oriented toward strategic needs and major scientific research plans defined in the Outline of the National Mid- to Long-Term Science and Technology Development Plan.

The world's first experimental superconducting tokomak magnetic fusion energy reactor is also known as the Experimental Advanced Superconducting Tokomak (EAST) and is mostly referred to as the "Artificial Sun." It was developed by the Institute of Plasma Physics of the Chinese Academy of Sciences, in Hefei City, Anhui Province.

Implementation of the construction of the National Scientific and Technological Basic Condition Platform to guarantee scientific and technological innovation. During the 11th Five-Year Plan period, while conforming to the policy of integrating, sharing, optimizing, and improving, the National Scientific and Technological Basic Condition Platform strengthened planning and top-level design, and further improved the platform through preferential selection, new construction, integration, and restructuring. The construction of a number of research and test centers focused on emerging disciplines, inter-disciplines, and unexplored fields by concentrating the government support on key national needs. This period also saw the launch of the construction of a number of key national laboratories and a network of national outdoor scientific observation and research stations. To promote the sharing of scientific data and literature resources, a digital scientific and technological platform has been built up, focusing on the informatization of scientific and technological conditions and resources. Several natural science and technology resources service platforms and national standards, measurements, and testing technology systems have also been set up.

This picture shows the longest bridge in China, the Hangzhou Bay Bridge. It has a total length of 36 km and was opened to traffic on May 1, 2008.

Implementation of policy-guided plans to create a new environment and mechanism for innovation. Policy-guided plans prescribed in the 11th Five-Year Plan are endowed with a clear policy orientation, focusing on the support for enterprise innovation, high-tech industrialization, and the transformation and popularization of scientific and technological achievements geared toward agriculture and rural areas, as well as the implementation of the Spark, Torch, and New Product programs.

The 863 Program and High-Tech Research

Introduction of the 863 Program

In China, the 863 Program is familiar to people in the scientific and industrial sectors, as well as scientists and the public.

The overall objectives of the 863 Program are to concentrate the talents in selected high-tech areas and bridge the gap of leading technologies of technologically advanced countries, propel scientific and technological progress in

THE ORIGIN OF THE 863 PROGRAM

On March 3, 1986, four senior scientists—Wang Daheng, Wang Ganchang, Yang Jiaxi, and Chen Fangyun—wrote a letter to the state leaders. In the letter, they proposed that China should track world-class developments to produce her own high-tech research and products. Deng Xiaoping attached great importance to this letter and personally instructed that the proposal should receive immediate attention. After a wide, far-reaching, and extremely strict scientific and technical demonstration, the Chinese government approved the High-tech Research Development Planning (or the 863 Program), which took China's high-tech research standards to new heights. As the plan was drawn according to the proposal made in March 1986, it was called 863. Since then, China's news media frequently uses the term 863, which has become an epoch-making symbol for China's entry into high-tech areas.

related areas, and cultivate a new generation of high-level technical personnel to prepare for the construction of a high-tech industry. In particular, the program seeks to create the conditions for further economic and social development at the end of the 20th century and the beginning of the 21st century, as well as ensuring national security.

The implementation of the 863 Program has created a number of high-tech industrial growth areas that not only promoted the development of China's high-tech research and high-tech industries, but also offered high-tech transformation of traditional industries.

High-tech Research in the 11th Five-Year Plan Period

In the 11th Five-Year Plan period, the 863 Program focused on the improvement of independent innovation in China's high-tech areas and R&D in cutting-edge technologies. It continued to emphasize on the intangible aspects of strategy, forward thinking, and vision. It also coordinated and deployed the integration and application of high-tech research and made full use of it in future technological developments.

This picture shows Deng Xiaoping penning a verse for the 863 Program: "Develop high-tech, realize modernization."

Overall Concept of the 863 Program Through exploration and research in cutting-edge technologies, the 863 Program strives to meet the needs of the country's future development. Cutting-edge technologies provide new methods and technical approaches to eliminate bottlenecks that constrained the areas such as national economy, social development, and national security. The program also promoted the use of core technologies and technical standards through ownership of intellectual property rights. The high-tech industries were rapidly developed through the strengthening and integration of high-tech research products and technology systems.

Using the results of high-tech applied research, emerging industries are nurtured to upgrade China's industrial technology and structural adjustment. The transformation of China's economy from resources-dependent to innovation-driven was thus accelerated and this, in turn, has effectively promoted and maintained economic and social development on the track of sound scientific development.

Overall Thrust of the 863 Program During the 11th Five-Year Plan period, the 863 Program focused on R&D in cutting-edge technologies for high-tech research areas such as information technology, biotechnology and medical technology, new materials technology, advanced manufacturing technology, advanced energy technology, resources and environmental technology, marine technology, modern agricultural technology, modern transportation technology, and earth observation and navigation technology. The program pushed forward the construction of high-tech R&D centers and platforms, and organized R&D according to the division of special programs and ordinary projects.

Special programs were encouraged to explore high-tech frontier areas and aimed to improve the innovation ability and acquisition of independent intellectual property rights. Major national projects concentrated on the strategic needs of the country and targeted the building of prototypes or major technical systems. Key projects had specific technical directions with core technologies or single strategic products as their ultimate goals. In this period, the 863 Program prioritized the organization and planning of 38 special programs along with other projects, and held onto the principle of launching a major new project once the preceding one was sufficiently mature, as well as initiating key projects in batches.

Strategic Focus of the 863 Program Information technology made it possible to master a number of cutting-edge technologies that could be exchanged and transferred with developed countries, giving China access to the supply chain of global information technology, thus creating competitive advantages in important areas.

The focus in biotechnology and medical technology was to achieve breakthroughs in several leading biotechnologies. Another aim of the program was to establish and optimize a biotechnology innovation system with Chinese characteristics, and lift China onto the ranks of advanced countries in the world of biotechnology.

New materials technology also delivered results in the form of design, evaluation, characterization, and fabrication of modern materials. Nano-materials research also resulted in the production of nano-materials and devices.

Advanced manufacturing technology developments are based on the key needs of the national economy and national defense. It involves the study of the key technologies, basic units, and integrated systems of advanced manufacturing.

Advanced energy technology vigorously developed energy-efficient technologies and the efficient conversion of coal, and actively developed new energy and renewable energy technologies to attain a diverse mix of energy resources.

Breakthroughs in resources and environmental technology focused on 100 key resources and environmental technologies. Efficient oil exploration and mining of rock minerals in difficult conditions were also developed, keeping the country's technical capacities in mind.

This picture, taken on November 28, 2008, shows China's first regional jet aircraft ARJ21-700 making its maiden flight in Shanghai.

In marine technology, the focus of the program was on improving the use of offshore resources and increasing the storage of deep-sea strategic resources, such as developing key technologies and major equipment for offshore oil fields in shallow waters, deep-water oil fields, and gas fields, gas hydrates, and the exploration and development of ocean seabed resources.

Modern agricultural technology made breakthroughs in the areas of agricultural biotechnology, agricultural information technology, intelligent technology in agriculture, and modern food biotechnology, as well as the creation of major products and the building of technical systems.

Modern transportation technology enhanced independent innovation capability in the manufacturing of automotive and other transportation equipment. It also strengthened capacity in assimilating, absorbing, and reverse engineering technology, core technologies, and realized the industrialization of her products.

The recent advances in earth observation and navigation technology of the country include programs such as the satellite navigation system, the lunar survey, and the man-in-space flight, as well as research on remote sensing, the terrestrial space information system and other technologies such as guided localization and advanced sensing.

Latest Progress of Some Cutting-edge Technologies In recent years, the major areas of concern for research on cutting-edge technologies have been restricted to difficult and popular issues that affect the national economy, people's livelihoods, and advanced problems in industrial development. Special plans have been made in the following aspects:

- R&D of key technology of energy-saving and emissions reduction;
- solving problems encountered in biotechnology and agricultural technology;
- upgrading of information technology;
- new materials technology;
- equipment manufacturing technology; and
- R&D on aerospace and marine technologies.

Breakthroughs have been achieved in a series of key technologies and a number of patents with independent intellectual property rights and significant results have been obtained. All these have improved the R&D capability and international competitiveness of China's high-tech capabilities, which laid the foundation for the development of high-tech industrialization.

In the research of petaflop high-performance computer architecture, a super-parallel structure and hybrid structure have been proposed for computing and processing, memory access, interconnected communications, and the input and output of balanced systems. The development of multi-core and many-core processors at home and abroad has received attention, and a system implementation plan, which is based on the latest processor, has been proposed. To date, the aggregate floating-point computing ability and total storage capacity of the China National Grid have exceeded 25.8 trillion times and 318 terabytes, respectively. The grid develops and deploys more than 100 high-performance computing and grid applications that involve many scientific research projects and engineering application areas of bio-information, materials, meteorology, astronomy, medicine, aerospace, transportation, finance, and chemistry.

In the research field of intelligent material design and advanced manufacturing technology, various nozzle gas flow fields and the mass distribution of metal particles after atomization have been studied to invent a new spray-forming technology for dual-scan atomization. A precise description on the growth form of deposited billets has been worked out through retroduction. Deposition models under different conditions of single jet, single-jet scans,

This picture shows a robot dancing in a contest organized during the Robotics Week held by the University of Science and Technology of China in Hefei City, Anhui Province.

dual jet, and dual-jet scans have been established. A temperature control method has been proposed to lower thermal stress in large deposited billets, reduce high thermal cracking, and reduce micro porosity. The GH738 high-temperature alloy and T15 high-speed steel spray-forming deposited billet have been successfully manufactured. The crystal grains of the billet are fine and uniform and their relative density surpasses 98%. Such high values of technical indicators have not been reported anywhere else in the world in this area of research.

Protection of Intellectual Property Rights and the Promotion of Scientific and Technological Innovation

The national innovation system is an institutional and organizational system in which science and technology resources are effectively integrated. Economy and technology is tightly integrated while robust interactions between technology innovation, knowledge innovation, national defense technology innovation, and science and technology intermediary services are promoted.

The Chinese government issued an initiative based on the Decisions on Accelerating Technology Innovation, Developing High-tech Research and Realizing Industrialization. The full deployment of a national innovation system hints at the emergence of a new reality where systemic innovation and scientific and technological innovation promote one another.

Strengthening of Intellectual Property Management

Science and technology is a strong influence on social developments in China. In modern society, creative work such as innovation and the development of science and technology, require a large amount of time, capital, and intellectual talent. Therefore, successful innovators should own the rights to their intellectual property and receive proportionate remuneration. In this way, their rights and incentives to innovate are protected and the impetus for innovation is thereby maintained. Enhancing the protection of intellectual property rights is a necessity in nurturing and improving independent innovation capabilities. The preservation of intellectual property is significant for encouraging independent innovation and the optimization of the innovation environment.

At the turn of the new century, the United States and Japan released their national strategies on intellectual property rights. Since then, the scope of intellectual property protection has expanded, and protection efforts have been

INTELLECTUAL PROPERTY SYSTEM

The intellectual property system is an important means of promoting scientific and technological innovation and managing and protecting intellectual property rights. This system endows intellectual innovators and innovation results with legal rights, preventing other people from using the results to gain benefits without permission from the inventors. As a result, it becomes an effective institutional agreement for protecting innovators' rights and benefits, as well as encouraging and stimulating inventors to continue to innovate.

strengthened. Intellectual property protection has developed from the protection of innovators' rights to a useful means for enterprises, industries, and countries to promote scientific and technological innovation and competitiveness, and has created enormous economic and social benefits. The Chinese government has made intellectual property protection an important strategic safeguard to drive scientific and technological innovation and create a culture of innovation, and has thus made great efforts to implement this decision. The Ministry of Science and Technology has adopted a series of policies and measures, and has made great progress in the work of intellectual property protection. The measures are as follows.

(1) During the 11th Five-Year Plan period, the country's patents system included three major areas of focus for science and technology work and for the development of intellectual property for scientific and technological innovation. Implementing the patents system was a strategic move for encouraging major scientific and technological innovations and is in line with the objectives of mastering core technologies and owning these intellectual property. Such a strategy is based on an in-depth analysis and understanding of the pattern and development trends in international technological and economic competition. It also involves the use of intellectual property to encourage innovation and accelerate the spread and utilization of innovation. By doing so, new breakthroughs in science and technology can be used to build a technology rights protection system supported by independent intellectual property.

(2) Perfecting intellectual property management for science and technology plans is critical. In 2002, the State Council forwarded the Provisions on Intellectual Property Management of National Scientific Research Results formulated by the Ministry of Science and Technology and the Ministry of Finance.

In 2003, the Ministry of Science and Technology issued the Provisions on Strengthening Intellectual Property Management of National Science and Technology Plans. These documents clearly stipulate that the acquisition, protection, and utilization of patent rights, new plant hybrid varieties, computer software copyrights, and technological secrets should be the major objectives for the implementation of science and technology plans. The intellectual property management responsibilities of science and technology project management units, project undertakers, and project participants in the process of project application, launching, accreditation, implementation, and acceptance are also defined in these documents. Besides these issues, the problem of the ambiguous division of responsibilities in the intellectual property management of China's science and technology projects has also been resolved. At present, intellectual property is included in the management system and project contracts of the 863 Program and other scientific research projects. The objectives and requirements for intellectual property output are clearly set out in the tender guide for major science and technology projects.

(3) Another key measure is the implementation of patent rights analysis in key areas of scientific and technological development to provide intellectual property measures for scientific and technological innovations. The Ministry of Science and Technology has set up a working group of intellectual property legal experts, technical experts, intellectual property practitioners, patent examiners, and information analysis institutions to work on such major projects as electric vehicles, functional genomics, water conservation and the dairy industry. These experts focus on special areas, collect and organize domestic and foreign patents and non-proprietary information to build up patent databases for these specific areas. They also put forward intellectual property objectives and measures for China to carry out scientific research in related areas through patent rights analysis and technical analysis.

(4) An intellectual property funding mechanism is to be built. Based on the stipulation that "intellectual property funds can be drawn from the funds of related national scientific research," that is stated in relevant documents of the Ministry of Science and Technology and the Ministry of Finance, subsidies have been set aside for patent applications for the National Transgenic Plant Research and Industrialization Project and New Plant Hybrid Varieties and the 863 Program international patent grants. This is to encourage and support patent applications for achievements made in national science and technology projects.

(5) The establishment of intellectual property alliances linking technical cooperation and intellectual property sharing is also given much emphasis. Taking the examples of national science and technology projects, the Ministry of Science and Technology was the main driver in the development of the 3G Mobile Communications Strategic Alliance and Electric Vehicle Strategic Alliance with other ministries.

(6) Intellectual property training and the improvement of the intellectual property management of scientific and technological innovation subjects have to be implemented. The focus is to improve the awareness of intellectual property among those who undertake national scientific and technological projects based on an analysis of the patent rights in related areas. It also looks at the peculiarities of intellectual property application and the protection of scientific and technological innovations in related areas, as well as provide critical guidance for project undertakers, project leaders, and R&D staff.

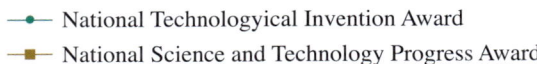

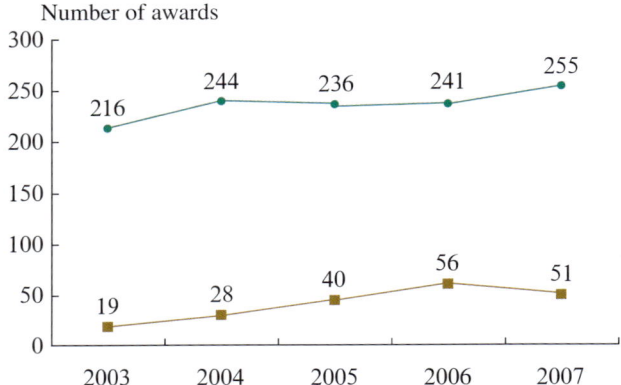

Source: *China Statistical Yearbook (2008)*

Status of National Technological Invention Award and National Science and Technology Progress Award (2003–2007)

In recent years, China has sped up her innovations in science and technology. In 2007, the number of recorded scientific and technological achievements totaled 34,170, an increase of 3,600 from 2003. The number of state technological awards and national science and technology progress awards has also grown.

New independent intellectual property has mushroomed and the number of applications and authorizations for patents of scientific and technological innovations has increased rapidly. China has the fourth largest number of patents in the world, just behind the United States, Japan, and the European Union, making China one of the leading intellectual property owners in the world. Chinese enterprises have ventured to more corners of the world and are paying more attention to the benefits of intellectual property. Consequently, the number of international patent applications submitted through the Patent Cooperation Treaty has risen by more than 30% since 2000. In 2006, China ranked 10th in the world in terms of applications. All these factors demonstrate that scientific and technological innovation ability and intellectual property protection awareness of Chinese enterprises have significantly improved.

Laws and Regulations Promoting Scientific and Technological Innovations

The amendment of the Science and Technology Progress Law and the issuance of the People's Republic of China Enterprise Income Tax Law have created a

Domestic and foreign authorizations for three types of patent application (1990–2007)

Patent Types (per application)	1990	1995	2000	2005	2006	2007
Total Inventions	3,838	3,393	12,683	53,305	57,786	67,948
Domestic	1,149	1,530	6,177	20,705	25,077	31,945
Foreign	2,689	1,863	6,506	32,600	32,709	36,003
Total Utility Models	16,952	30,471	54,743	79,349	107,655	150,036
Domestic	16,744	30,195	54,407	78,137	106,312	148,391
Foreign	208	276	336	1,212	1,343	1,645
Total Designs	1,798	11,200	37,919	81,349	102,561	133,798
Domestic	1,411	9,523	34,652	72,777	92,471	121,296
Foreign	387	1,677	3,267	8,572	10,090	12,502
Total Authorized	**22,588**	**45,064**	**105,345**	**214,003**	**268,002**	**351,782**

Source: *China Statistical Yearbook (2008)*

sound legal environment for improving China's independent innovation ability and the building up of an innovative culture.

Science and Technology Progress Law   The People's Republic of China Science and Technology Progress Law was revised and passed during the 31st Meeting of the 10th National People's Congress on December 29, 2007. The revised law came into effect on July 1, 2008.

The revised law supports existing basic research projects, high-tech research and high-tech industrialization, agricultural technology R&D, and the promotion and protection of the legal rights and interests of science and technology manpower, as well as the improvement of the efficiency of R&D institutes. It fully capitalizes on China's successful experience in scientific and technological development and reform. Targeting problems that constrain scientific and technological progress and linking up the needs to strengthen independent innovation, this law makes a series of institutional and systemic innovations in a number of areas as follows.

The law clarifies the objectives, policies, and strategies for China's scientific and technological development. It brings into its realm the task of enhancing independent innovation and building an innovation-oriented country. The law notes that "the country follows the scientific concept of development and implements the strategy of revitalizing the country through science and education." It defines the government's responsibilities in promoting scientific and technological progress and further stipulates that government funds should be primarily invested in the construction of scientific and technological needs and infrastructure, fundamental research, and leading-edge technology research that play an important role in economic construction and social development. The law highlights the dominant position of enterprise innovation and subjects the enterprises to the integration of commercial exploitation and research to break new grounds in the building of a national innovation system. The law improves incentives for scientific and technological innovation and encourages the public sharing of scientific and technological resources.

Related Laws and Regulations on Science and Technology The People's Republic of China Enterprise Income Tax Law was passed during the Fifth Meeting of the 10th National People's Congress on March 16, 2007, and came into force on January 1, 2008. This law unifies tax rates levied on domestic and foreign enterprises by a singular benchmark rate of 25%. At the same time, in order to encourage the development of high-tech industries, it institutes a levy of 15% on all high-tech enterprises.

In 2007, technology rules and regulations with local characteristics were drawn up around the country to encourage independent innovation. The

During the 11th China International Software Expo, the participants responded warmly to the petition campaign of "Insist on Using Genuine Software."

governments of Shanghai, Shenzhen, Zhuhai, and Ji'nan formulated and amended their provisions to fund science and technology.

First, there was to be a substantial increase in funding for awards and individual award amounts. Second, the ultimate goal of the awards was adjusted, moving away from simply funding projects to an overall funding for projects, teams, and individuals. Third, the assessment procedures for technology awards were fine-tuned. For example, in Shenzhen, a system based on recommendations was replaced by free applications. Fourth, the public was encouraged to set up its own awards. In Shenzhen, for example, public awards registered and recorded with the government do qualify for a certain amount of governmental financial support. The government of Guizhou drew up the Guizhou Province High-tech Industry Development Regulation through which it set aside special funds for high-tech industry development and supported the development of high-tech enterprises. It is also stated in the regulation that high-tech enterprises should invest at least 5% of their total sales as funding for enterprise technology innovation.

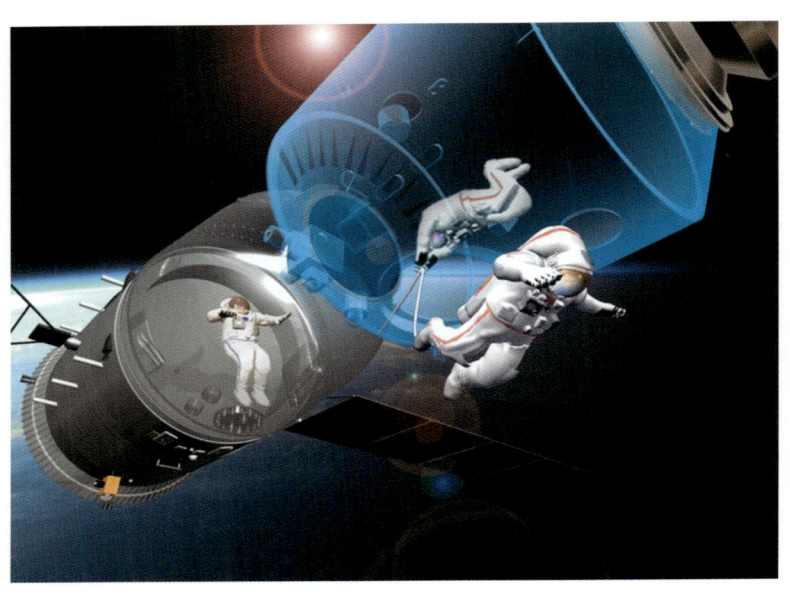

Chapter 4

....

Fruits of High-Tech Industrialization

A series of scientific and technological activities, such as the Torch Program, the National Major New Product Program, the Technology Innovation Fund for Technology-oriented Small and Medium-sized Enterprises, and the High-Tech Industrialization Project aimed at promoting high-tech have seen continuous progress and have effectively sustained China's rapid economic development.

Major Areas and Achievements of High-Tech Industrialization

Major Areas of High-tech Industrialization

In the National Economic and Social Development Section of the 11th Five-Year Plan, the electronics manufacturing industry, bio-industry, aerospace industry, and new materials industry have been earmarked as key concerns. The plan also calls for the promotion of a shift in the high-tech industry, moving from the focus on processing and assembly-based manufacturing to one that is focused on independent R&D while pushing forward the commercialization of independent innovation results, as well as the development of a number of leading industries with core competitiveness, industrial centers with outstanding ability in attracting talent, multinational high-tech enterprises, and well-known brands with independent intellectual property.

Electronics Manufacturing The development of electronics manufacturing conforms to the general trend of digitalization, networking and intelligence, the development of core industries such as integrated circuits, software, and new materials, and the focus on the cultivation of information-based industries such as optical communications, wireless communications, high-performance computing, and network equipment. Research centers were also created to develop the software, microelectronics, and optoelectronics industries and boost the formation of an optoelectronics industry "chain." There are also efforts to boost the key technologies of the information industry and enhance innovation and competitiveness in order to expand the industry "chain."

Bio-industry A goal in bio-industry is to make good use of China's unique advantages in biological resources and technology and to take into consideration the key areas of health care, agriculture, environmental protection, energy, and new materials, as well as to prioritize the R&D of biomedical, bio-agriculture, bio-energy, and bio-manufacturing. The development of this industry also includes carrying out bio-industry special projects to seek breakthroughs in

This picture shows researchers sequencing protein structures in the gene laboratory of Shanghai Fudan-Zhangjiang Bio-Pharmaceutical Co., Ltd.

core technologies and important product developments, while improving market access, protecting unique bio-resources, and safeguarding bio-security.

Aerospace Industry The aerospace industry adheres to the policies of combining local and foreign resources, integrating military and civilian efforts, combining self-development and international cooperation. Its aims also include the development of new regional aircraft, large aircraft, helicopters, advanced engines and avionics. In addition, sub-contracted production has been expanded to advance aerospace industrialization. It also seeks to shift the industry's focus from being experiment- and application-oriented to being business- and service-oriented, developing and utilizing communications, navigation, and remote sensing satellites to build up an aerospace industry "chain" that encompasses space, ground, end-user product manufacturing, and operational services.

New Materials Industry This industry focuses on the needs of the information, biological, aerospace, large-sized equipment, and new energy industries. It also develops industrial clusters for special functional materials, high-performance structural materials, nano-materials, composite materials, and green energy-efficient materials, while setting up and improving the new material innovation system.

Introduction to the Development of High-tech Industrialization

In recent years, China's high-tech industry has maintained rapid development and the competitive power of its high-tech products in international markets has improved. In 2007, the industrial output value of high-tech enterprises totaled RMB 5,046.1 billion, an increase of 20.2% over the previous year. The total added value was RMB 1,162.1 billion, an increase of 15.6%. Remarkable results were made in promoting the transformation of high-tech achievements.

Manpower and Funding for Science and Technology In 2007, there were around 480,000 science and technology personnel in China's high-tech industries and 340,000 of these were scientists and engineers. The total amount of money allocated for science and technology funds topped RMB 94.7 billion, with RMB 81 billion receiving investments from enterprises, accounting for 85.5% of the total. Expenditure on product development was RMB 65.2 billion. Of the RMB 21.1 billion spent on high-tech industry technology transformation, RMB 13.1 billion was spent on technology introduction, RMB 1.4 billion on the adaptation of imported technology, and RMB 1.1 billion was used for the purchases of local technology.

The number of enterprise-level science and technology institutions reached 2,217 with more than 240,000 scientific and technological personnel.

The expenditures of these institutions also reached RMB 47.8 billion. In terms of industries, funds raised for scientific and technological activities of electronics and communications equipment manufacturing took up 57.1% of the total. The respective proportion of funds for scientific and technological activities in computer and office equipment manufacturing, the pharmaceutical industry, the aerospace industry, and medical equipment and instrument manufacturing amounted to 15.5%, 13.4%, 7.6%, and 6.3%, respectively.

Patents Registered from the High-tech Industry   In 2007, the number of patent applications by the high-tech industry amounted to 34,446, with the industry having sole ownership for 13,386 patents. Among the patents held by the industry, 6,532 were in the electronics and communications equipment manufacturing industry, or 48.8% of the total, and pharmaceutical manufacturers held 2,482, or 18.5% of the total. The electronics and office equipment manufacturing industry, aerospace industry, and medical equipment and

DEVELOPMENT OF CHINA'S HIGH-TECH INDUSTRY IN 2007

In 2007, the output value of electronics and communications equipment manufacturing reached RMB 2,508.8 billion, accounting for 49.7% of the total output. The output value of computer and office equipment manufacturing totaled RMB 1,485.9 billion, or 29.4% of the total output. The output value of the pharmaceutical industry was RMB 6,362 billion, or 12.6% of the total. The total exports for China's high-tech products reached US$3,478 billion, an increase of 23.6% over the previous year, accounting for 28.6% of total exports.

In 2007, the high-tech industry received a total investment of RMB 3,484 billion, while the amount of new fixed assets reached RMB 1,958 billion. Out of the 7,702 construction projects, a total of 4,190 were new projects and 2,729 were finished projects.

In terms of completed investments, the electronics and communications equipment manufacturing industry received RMB 1,871 billion, accounting for 53.7% of total investments. Investments in the pharmaceutical industry reached RMB 828 billion or 23.8% of the total. The amount for medical equipment and instrument manufacturing was RMB 298 billion, 8.5% of the total.

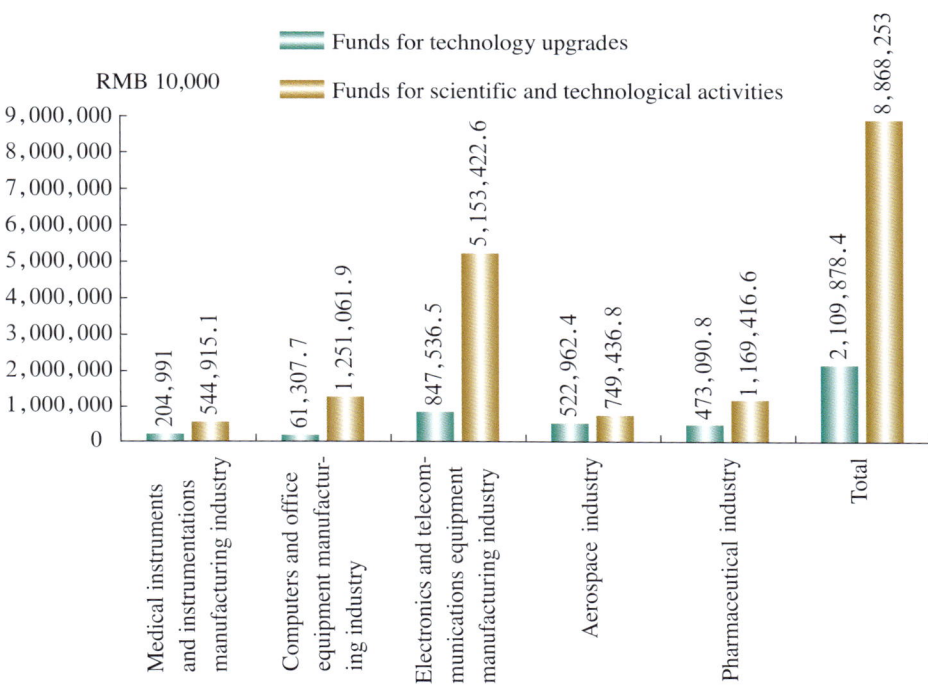

Source: *China Statistical Yearbook (2008)*

Investments in scientific and technological activities of large and medium-sized enterprises in the high-tech industry in 2007

instrumentation manufacturing industry owned 3,210, 270, and 892 patents, respectively, with each proportion at 24.5%, 2%, and 6.7%, respectively.

Within the electronics and communications equipment manufacturing industry, large-scale enterprises owned 4,829 patents, 2.8 times the number of patents held by medium-sized enterprises. Large enterprises in the electronics and office equipment manufacturing industry owned 2,532 patents, 3.7 times the number held by medium-sized enterprises. In the aerospace industry, large enterprises possessed more patents than medium-sized enterprises, while the number of patents owned by large enterprises was significantly lower than that of medium-sized enterprises in pharmaceutical manufacturing, medical equipment, and instrumentation manufacturing.

In the pharmaceutical manufacturing and aerospace industries, the number of patents owned by state-owned enterprises and state-holding enterprises was higher than that owned by foreign-funded enterprises. However, in the medical equipment and instrumentation manufacturing industry, the electronics and communications manufacturing industry, and the electronics

This picture shows a composite shield machine model designed and developed by the China Railway Tunnel Group Co. Ltd.

and office equipment manufacturing industry, state-owned and state-holding enterprises held fewer patents than foreign-funded enterprises.

Development of High-tech Industrial Development Zones

The Chinese government began to approve the establishment of national high-tech industrial development zones in 1998. Under the policy instruction and support from the state, the construction of high-tech industrial development zones in China witnessed continuous progress.

The number of enterprises in development zones continued to grow, the progress of regional congregation was further accelerated, and the formation of industrial clusters was sped up. By the end of 2007, the number of national high-tech industrial development zones had increased to 54, up from 27 in 1990. The number of enterprises in these zones grew from 1,600 to over 480,000, and the number of practitioners increased to 6,502,000 from 123,000. The total income and output in 2007 respectively topped RMB 5.5 trillion and RMB 4.4 trillion, 726 times and 769 times the totals in 1990. High-tech industrial parks and economic and technological development zones became an important gathering place for China's high-tech industry.

During the 10th Five-Year Plan, the Ministry of Science and Technology drew up the Decision on Further Supporting the Development of National High-Tech Industrial Development Zones and the National High-Tech Industrial Development Zone Technology Innovation Outline, which provided important guidelines for new ventures in high-tech industrial zones and took these zones to a new stage of development.

Expenditures for Scientific and Technological Activities In 2007, funds raised for scientific and technological activities in high-tech enterprises totaled RMB 217.99 billion, and scientific and technological expenditure totaled RMB 216.35 billion. The amount spent on R&D was RMB 134.88 billion, about 3.0% of the products' sales.

Science and Technology Manpower In 2007, there were 6,502,000 practitioners in high-tech enterprises. Of these, 2,753,000 had a college education, or 42.3% of the total. Among the practitioners, 1.25 million had bachelor degrees, 216,000 had master degrees, and 29,000 held doctorates. There were 897,000 management-level practitioners, accounting for 13.8% of the total. In 2007, enterprises in high-tech zones recruited 263,000 fresh college graduates.

Output of Scientific and Technological Activities In 2007, the output value of new products in high-tech zones reached RMB 1,179.6 billion. New product sales reached RMB 12,216.3 billion, accounting for 26.9% of the total product sales. The amount of new product exports reached US$39.06 billion, 22.6% of total exports from high-tech zones.

FYI

FOR YOUR
INFORMATION

BASIC SET-UP OF NEW VENTURES IN NATIONAL HIGH-TECH ZONES

First, there was a change in the development mode from extensional development, which focused on investments and incentives, to connotative development, that mainly relied on scientific and technological innovation.

Second, there was a shift in focus from construction such as infrastructure, to services that stressed the optimal allocation of scientific and technological resources and white-knight services.

> Third, there was a change in product sales; moving from the original focus on the domestic market to exploring international markets. Fourth, there was an initiative to shift the industry from the model of small and scattered industries to one that is concentrated on joint strengths, enhanced integration, and the development of specialized and leading industries.
>
> Fifth, the existing mechanism that emphasized gradual and accumulative reform changed to a new one that was able to adapt to the requirements of the socialist market economy and the development laws of the high-tech industry.

In 2007, the number of patent applications in high-tech zones was 55,252 with 29,166 invention patents, 18% of all patent applications from enterprises throughout the country. The number of granted patents in high-tech zones reached a total of 24,522, of which licensed invention patents amounted to 7,658 or 16% of the total invention patents licensed to enterprises nationwide.

By 2007, enterprises in high-tech zones held a cumulative total of 49,680 invention patents. Foreign-invested enterprises took up the largest proportion with 13,677, limited liability companies held 12,594, and incorporated companies held 6,733. In high-tech zones, the number of invention patents possessed for every one million people was 76.4.

Key National Science and Technology Projects

Since the reform and opening up in 1978, China has resolved a large number of key technological problems in national economic and social development through scientific and technological research and projects, introduction of new technology, and transformations. The overall scientific and technological strength of the country has been greatly enhanced, and has taken a leading position among developing countries. However, the tracking and imitation-based technology development mode has been slow to adapt to the current accelerated trends of upgrading China's technology.

In December 2001, to accelerate the changes in China's technology development strategy from tracking and imitation to independent innovation and leapfrogging technological development, the Ministry of Science and Technology decided to carry out 12 key national science and technology projects during the 10th Five-Year Plan period. Under the guiding ideology of "forge

This picture shows a part of the Shanghai Zhangjiang High-Tech Zone.

ahead when you know the right way" and the principle of "focus on key projects only," every project has placed special emphasis on cross-sector and interdisciplinary technology integration to achieve major technological breakthroughs.

In 2006, the Ministry of Science and Technology released 16 national science and technology projects for the 11th Five-Year Plan period. Key science and technology projects have special significance in the construction of an innovation-oriented country with national strategic objectives. These projects organize and carry out major strategic product development, key common technology research and major construction projects through breakthroughs in core technologies and resource integration. They are the top priority for China's scientific and technological development in the next 15 years. These key projects, set with clear objectives, greatly influence and drive economic and social development, national defense, and scientific and technological development, and are of tremendous strategic and symbolic significance.

Overall Plan

In the National Science and Technology Development Ninth Five-Year Plan (1996–2000) and 2010 Long-term Development Plan, five principles were put forward for the implementation of key science and technology projects.

First, closely connect major needs in economic and social development to foster strategic industries that have independent intellectual property that can promote the improvement of the innovation capability of enterprises. Second, focus on key common technologies that have an overall influence that provide a strong impetus to the improvement of industrial competitiveness. Third, resolve major bottlenecks that constrain economic and social development. Fourth, embody the principle of combining military and civilian technology and integrating the armed forces, which is strategically significant for national security and the enhancement of comprehensive strength. Fifth, be in line with China's national conditions and focus on her national strength.

According to the principles mentioned above and the current focus on developing a high-tech industry, traditional industries need to be upgraded; bottlenecks need to be removed in national economic and social development; public health need to be improved; and national security has to be beefed up. In addition, 16 major science and technology projects have been confirmed. These projects cover strategic industries such as information and biology, critical and urgent problems such as energy resources, the environment, public health, and dual-use technology, and national defense technology.

These projects include core electronics, high-end general chips and basic software, ULSI manufacturing technology and its complete process, next-generation broadband wireless mobile communications, high-end CNC machine tools and technology, the development of large-scale gas and oil fields and coal-bed methane, large-scale advanced pressurized water reactors and high temperature gas-cooled reactor nuclear power stations, water pollution control and treatment, the cultivation of new varieties of genetically modified organisms, the development of major new drugs, the prevention and control of major infectious diseases such as AIDS and viral hepatitis, as well as projects in developing large aircrafts, high-resolution earth observation systems, manned space flights, and lunar exploration projects.

Organization and Management

Under the leadership of the State Council, joint coordination and integration of departments in these major projects have been highlighted. In every project, there is a leading group made up of related departments and units. Related departments, local governments, and enterprises will lead the organization and implementation of the project.

A Leadership System to Organize and Coordinate Bodies and Corresponding Working Mechanisms Under the leadership of the State Council, the National Science and Technology Education Leading Group is in charge of coordinating and guiding key projects. In the Fourth Meeting of the National Science and

The picture shows a model of the first Chinese-made large aircraft—the C919, which is currently under development. This project was officially launched in May 2008, after the Commercial Aircraft Corporation of China, Ltd. (COMAC) was established.

Technology Education Leading Group held on May 29, 2006, the leadership system for major projects was established, which marked the beginning of a comprehensive start-up phase in the organization and implementation of key projects.

As the department in charge of national science and technology affairs, the Ministry of Science and Technology, together with the National Development and Reform Commission and the Ministry of Finance, took responsibility for program demonstration, overall balance, assessment and acceptance, and the studying and formulating of supporting policies for the implementation of key projects. The three departments have set up the Three-sector Joint Meeting System and the Major Project Inter-ministerial Coordinating System. The Ministry of Science and Technology has established a Major Project Office and an internal liaison system to push the implementation of those key projects.

Initiate the Research and Formulation of Implementation Management Provisions for Key Projects Key projects have been the highlight of science and technology planning system reform for the 11th Five-Year Plan period. Their organization and implementation modes are significantly different from those in other former plans. The implementation of key projects is divided into three stages: implementation; construction, organization and implementation;

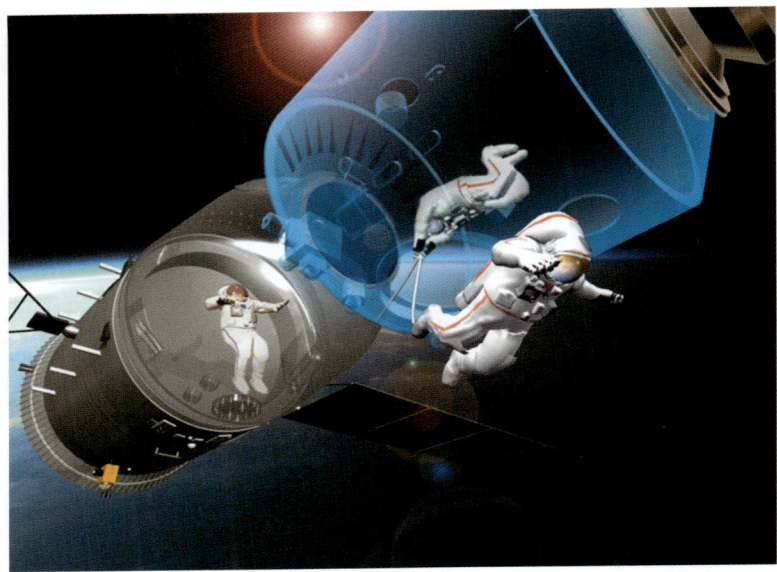

Plans for a manned space flight and lunar exploration is one of the key projects outlined in the 11th Five-Year Plan period.

and assessment and acceptance. The Ministry of Science and Technology deployed forces to carry out research and draft relevant regulations, which laid a foundation for the organization and implementation of other key projects.

Influence of High-Tech Industrialization on China's Economy

Economic Globalization and High-tech Industrialization

Since the 1990s, economic globalization has developed rapidly. Driven by information technology, a new economy has emerged. It is based on the information revolution, with aims for the global market, and constantly adjusts and optimizes its industrial structure. As a high-tech industry, it is of strong relevance and so, represents a pushing force. It has the potential for high growth and profits and has become the leading sector within the industrial structure. It is an important impetus for upgrading the industrial structure.

Nowadays, the high-tech industry and its industrial clusters have become the main source of economic growth and knowledge-intensive technology products increasingly take up a larger proportion of international trade. Consequently, it would be more and more pressing for the country to exchange its low technology, low value-added, resource-intensive and labor-intensive products for high-tech, high value-added, and knowledge-intensive products. By exploiting its advantages, China can actively seize the opportunity for development to find its proper place in the world in the high-tech industry by participating in the process of economic globalization. The nation now looks to the high-tech industry as its leading industry to boost the formation and development of high-tech industrial clusters, to accelerate the adjustment and upgrading of industrial structure, and to narrow the gap with developed countries.

In August 1988, the government initiated the National High-Tech Industrialization Development Program, known as the Torch Program. The program highlighted the importance of the establishment of high-tech industry development zones and high-tech innovation service centers.

In the past 20 years, the rapid development of high-tech industry has propelled the enlargement of China's high-tech product imports and exports. According to official statistics, in 2007, the total imports and exports of China's high-tech products reached US$634.8 billion, 111.3 times the total in 1986 (there are no statistics prior to 1986). Exports totaled US$3,478 billion and imports US$2,870 billion, which are 484.4 times and 57.6 times the totals in 1986, respectively.

ACHIEVEMENTS OF THE TORCH PROGRAM

In the past two decades since the Torch Program was implemented, China's high-tech industrialization and relevant environment construction have experienced rapid development. China's science and technology have been effectively integrated into economic growth.

In the past 20 years, the Torch Program has played a major congregating, leading, and influencing role in improving regional and enterprise independent innovation capability, and the construction of an innovation-oriented culture. It has successfully explored a policy environment and an operating mechanism and system for high-tech industrialization with unique Chinese characteristics. It has nurtured entrepreneurial culture and innovation awareness to develop high-tech industrialization. It has also trained a large army of entrepreneurs and has promoted the establishment of many high-tech enterprises that are the backbone of China's revitalization.

In 2007, there were 60,000 high-tech enterprises. R&D investment in these enterprises accounted for about 45% of the total R&D investment in the country. Take high-tech zones as an example: 605 listed enterprises have emerged from these zones in the past 20 years. The number of high-tech enterprises whose annual revenue exceeded RMB 100 million surpassed 5,000; and of these, more than 90 enterprises achieved annual revenues of over RMB 5 billion, while that of 83 enterprises surpassed RMB 10 billion.

A shift from a deficit of US$4.27 billion in 1986 to a surplus of US$60.8 billion was realized in imports and exports. The export of high-tech products is playing an increasingly significant role in China's foreign trade. In 2007, exports of high-tech products took up 28.6% of total merchandise exports, increasing by 26.3 basis points from the 2.3% figure recorded in 1986.

High-tech Zones as an Important Driver for Regional Development

On a global scale, science and technology industrial parks have played a fundamental role, since their inception in the 1950s, in the promotion

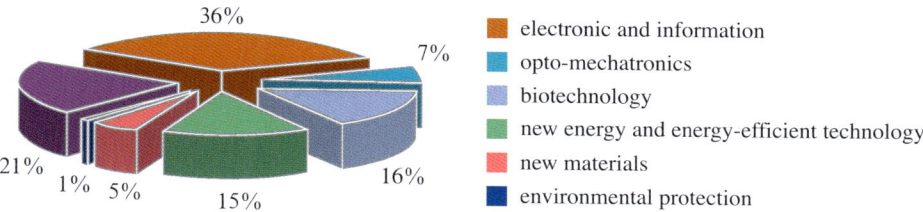

36%

7%

21%

1% 5%

15%

16%

- electronic and information
- opto-mechatronics
- biotechnology
- new energy and energy-efficient technology
- new materials
- environmental protection

Source: *Chinese High-Tech Industry Statistics (2008)*

Distribution of technology product sales of high-tech zone enterprises in 2007

and transformation of scientific and technological results, the nurturing of innovation-oriented high-tech industries and entrepreneurs, bringing about a new technological revolution in emerging industries, and boosting the new economy. They have become an effective means for the country and various regions to realize high-tech industrialization, thus promoting economic growth and sustainable social development.

In May 1988, Beijing Zhongguancun Science Park, the first national high-tech industrial development zone in China, was established. For the past 20 years, China's high-tech zones have undergone rapid development and become an important force in national economic construction.

Optimization of Industrial Structure The industrial structure of China's high-tech zones has been constantly optimized and a large industrial development trend of obvious characteristics and clusters has been principally formed. A series of industrial clusters such as information technology in Beijing, micro-electronics in Shanghai, communications technology in Shenzhen, optoelec-tronics and automotives in Changchun, communications and software in Xi'an, biomedical technology in Chengdu, communications equipment in Hangzhou, optoelectronics in Wuhan, and green energy in Tianjin have taken shape or are under construction. The establishment of high-tech industrial belts in the Yangtze River Delta, Pearl River Delta, and Bohai Sea Rim Zone play signifi-cant supporting roles in the implementation of major national strategies, such as the development of western China, the revitalization of Northeast China's traditional industrial hubs, and the economic rise in central China.

Contributions to Regional Economies National high-tech zones have played a significant role in promoting the economic development of the cities in which they are located. The proportion of industrial added value that high-tech enterprises produce in relation to the total added value of the city they are located in continues to grow. Official statistics from 2006 show that the proportion of added value contributed by 21 high-tech zones exceeded 30%.

Proportion of added value of high-tech zones			
High-Tech Zones	Proportion of Added Value (%)	High-Tech Zones	Proportion of Added Value (%)
Yangling	94.2	Jilin	45
Xi'an	62.2	Weihai	44.6
Zibo	51	Haikou	41.9
Hefei	46.6	Chengdu	39.5
Baoji	46.1	Zhuhai	39
Changzhou	46.1	Shijiazhuang	30
Nanning	33.6	Taiyuan	33.4
Xiangfan	33.5	Guilin	32.6
Huizhou	32.3	Changchun	31.7
Changsha	30.6	Wuhan	30.5
Zhongguancun Science Park	38.9		

As for the proportion of GDP produced by national high-tech zones to that of the local city, 11 high-tech zones surpassed 20%. These high-tech zones were found in Yangling, Zibo, Weihai, Zhuhai, Weifang, Changzhou, Jilin, Xi'an, Suzhou, Hefei, and the Zhongguancun Science Park.

Resource Conservation Green and clean production is advocated in national high-tech zones, and polluting enterprises are strictly controlled. Remarkable success has been achieved in promoting the environmental management certification and construction of demonstration zones. All these have greatly contributed to the development of a resource-saving and environmentally friendly society. In 2007, the comprehensive energy consumption of the average output of RMB 10,000 for industrial enterprises over a designated size in national high-tech zones was 0.198 tons of standard coal. The comprehensive energy consumption of the average added value was 0.51 tons of standard coal per RMB 10,000, about 40% of the average standard of the country's industrial enterprises of a certain size.

Enhanced international influence A strategy of internationalization has been actively implemented in national high-tech zones. The degree of opening up of high-tech zones continues to rise and their international influence has been enhanced. Most national high-tech zones have made progress in the absorption of international resources, active participation in international divisions of labor, and seizing opportunities in international markets. The export of high-tech products has seen continuous growth and there has been an increase in the interest of some multinational corporations in transnational talent introduced by high-tech enterprises.

In October 2007, Plant No. 1 of Century Epitech Co., Ltd., a large-scale compound semiconductor industry base, formally began its operation in Shenzhen.

THE ROLE OF HIGH-TECH ZONES

While the independent innovation ability of high-tech zones has been improved, the economic development of surrounding areas has been propelled by the radiating and stimulating effect of these zones. By managing the township construction of supporting science and technology industrial parks and jointly building the Wuxi-Xinyi industrial zone with Xuzhou City, the Wuxi High-Tech Zone followed a development path of mutual interaction and a win-win situation between the high-tech zone, its surrounding areas, and less developed areas.

The Luoyang High-Tech Zone, making use of the county's ample mineral resources and rich variety of Chinese herbal medicines, signed a contract with Luanchuan County and built up an industrial base that focused on minerals finishing, plant extraction, and local specialty processing. The Weifang High-Tech Zone takes Fenghuang Mountain High-Tech Industrial Park as its radiating zone, and has built a technological incubator with outstanding talent and technological advantages to improve the amount and size of enterprises in Fenghuang Mountain High-Tech Industrial Park.

Software outsourcing services undertaken by high-tech enterprises have doubled, and progress has been achieved in foreign investments. A number of renowned science and technology parks such as Zhongguancun Science Park and Shanghai Zhangjiang High-Tech Park have attracted attention from the world's science and technology industry. In 2006, the amount of actual investment from foreign corporations in 53 national high-tech zones reached US$76.08 billion, which was 11.3% of the US$673.38 billion of foreign investments actually used by China in the same period.

Joint Creation of a Harmonious Society While maintaining rapid development in science and technology and the economy, high-tech zones have helped to build up emerging urban communities, successfully resolving the problems of employment, livelihood protection, and the development of social undertakings. By building first-class social support environments for habitation, education, and medical treatment, these zones bring tangible benefits to people living in and nearby the zones.

In the process of construction, the Zhongshan High-Tech Zone always prioritized benefits to farmers, protected the property of each household, and ensured a job for every farmer of working age, as well as food rations,

This picture shows Beijing's Zhongguancun Plaza on Christmas Eve.

a pension, and a house for each farmer. The Chengdu High-Tech Zone raised its financial investment and laid more emphasis on education and health, aided the needy, and provided labor and social security. Besides these initiatives, it also provided services in civil affairs, birth control, social security, employment, and training to benefit the local public. This zone has also improved the basic quality of life for its inhabitants and put in efforts to solve the problem of employment for college students and migrant workers.

Chapter 5

Science Education and Activities

The western concept of "popular science" is known in China as "science and technology popularization," or "science popularization." Science popularization in China is a multi-layered, three-dimensional undertaking. Compared with the general understanding of science in western countries, it includes richer content such as the popularization of scientific knowledge, advocacy of scientific methods, the spread of scientific thought and the promotion of the scientific spirit. Since the establishment of the People's Republic of China, science education has been regarded as a part of public education. The government attaches great importance to it, which can be shown in the construction of many science education sites and facilities, and the organization of various science education activities.

Science Popularization in Education

Management and Coordination of Science Popularization

During the early days of the People's Republic of China, the government set up the Department of Science and Technology Popularization under the Ministry of Culture to lead and manage national science education. Thereafter, special science education management agencies were founded in other departments and local authorities.

The government invested considerable funds in building venues for national science education. Both the central government and local governments set up special science education funds to support science popularization. At present, funds for science education come mainly from government funding. In all walks of life, including the science and technology sectors, media and publishing, urban communities, and enterprises all actively engage in science education.

National Science Administration   The Chinese government has adopted a centralized path of management and coordination with regards to science education. According to the People's Republic of China Science Popularization Law, the Ministry of Science and Technology is in charge of planning for the nation's science education and carrying out policy guidance, supervision, and inspection.

In April 1996, the National Joint Conference System for Science Education was set up. The Ministry of Science and Technology was made the managing body while the Department of Central Propaganda and the China Association of Science and Technology were designated as deputy managing bodies. Members of the system dealing with science education include departments under the central government, the State Council, and other mass organizations. Later on, local joint conference systems for science education were also established in various parts of China. These systems have provided an institutional guarantee for effectively engaging all kinds of organizations and bodies in popularizing science.

In every system of the State Council, all ministries and commissions carry out science popularization activities based on their key functions. The Ministry of Science and Technology established a Science Education Office under the Department of Policy and Reform. The function of this office is to draft national science education policies and regulations, to organize and coordinate key national science popularization activities, and to improve and implement science and technology communications systems. The institutions under the Ministry of Education, the Department of Basic Education, the Department of Professional and Adult Education, the Department of Science and Technology, the Department of Normal Education and the Department of Sports, Sanitation, and the Arts participate in science and technology education and science popularization based on their own respective functions.

The responsibilities of the Ministry of Health include carrying out comprehensive health education, providing guidance for the implementation of Primary Health Care Programs and maternal and child health special techniques, as well as guiding the popularization and application of medical

This picture, taken in August 2002, shows Professor Stephen Hawking receiving a warm welcome when he visited Beijing.

science and technology achievements. The Ministry of Agriculture has also played an important role in rural science education. Its Department of Science and Technology Education is responsible for the popularization of agricultural scientific and technological knowledge, and the promotion of agricultural technologies. In addition, the Ministry of Agriculture actively supports the science popularization of the China Agricultural Association.

Institutions for Science Education Although the China Association of Science and Technology (CAST) is only a public science and technology organization, it has played an important role in China's scientific and technological development. The main function of the association is to popularize science and technology. Since the founding of the People's Republic of China, it has made prominent contributions to science popularization through science and technology activities. In the Science and Technology Popularization Law, it clearly states that CAST will be the key player in science popularization, and is responsible for the organization and implementation of science popularization.

The Department of Science and Technology Popularization was set up under CAST to take charge of science popularization within the association. Among 167 national institutes affiliated to CAST, 138 have each set up a working committee for science popularization. The association has become a science popularization organization with systems ranging from central to local institutions.

The Chinese Academy of Sciences (CAS) is also an important department in science popularization. Its major responsibilities in science popularization include:

- leverage on the academy's advantages in high-tech talents and advanced research facilities to strengthen relations among scientific research institutes, and scientific and technological personnel with the public;
- mobilizing and organizing scientists and scientific and technological personnel to propagate scientific and technological knowledge through various modes;
- encouraging R&D institutes to organize public tours of the laboratories;
- popularizing science through lectures and visits;
- fully demonstrating the academy's advantages in the number of its intellectuals, facilities, and resources; and
- publicizing timely and recent scientific and technological results of the academy.

The academy also established a Science Popularization Leading Group and CAS Science Popularization Office. The leading group and the office are responsible for the science popularization of CAS and the active implementation of scientific activities.

The All-China Women's Federation set up the Department of Women's Development. The functions of this department in science popularization include:

- instructing women's organizations around the country to organize cultural and technological training and professional skills training for women;
- mobilizing and organizing women to participate in poverty alleviation, developing the western region of China, and eco-environmental construction;
- encouraging women living in rural areas to achieve prosperity through science and technology;
- guiding women's organizations to organize activities related to campaigns such as "two learning and two comparison"[1] and "nation-building by Chinese women."

The functions of the Children's Work Department in science popularization include carrying out work to promote girls' healthy development, participating

---

[1] Learning about culture; learning about technology, and comparing achievements; comparing contributions.

in the promotion of extra-curricular education, and coordinating and mobilizing the public to create a good environment for children's healthy development.

In addition, there are special departments under the Federation of Trade Unions and the Communist Youth League that organize science popularization activities for workers and young people.

Sites and Facilities

Sites and facilities for popularizing science and public education are vital. By the end of 2006, there were 859 science popularization sites across the country. Each site covers an area of over 500 sq. m. The total floor area of science and technology halls, science and technology museums reached 3,554,300 sq. m and science galleries added another 1,278,200 sq. m. The total number of visitors that same year topped 33,070,200. There were also 2,016 science and technology education centers and 134,500 science-themed art galleries.[2] There were 47,100 science and technology special activity rooms in urban communities and another 235,000 located in rural areas.

Science and Technology Museums Science and technology museums are comprehensive science popularization sites. These museums are especially dedicated to exhibition, training, and experimental education.

The China Museum of Science and Technology is managed by the China Association for Science and Technology and is China's sole national comprehensive science and technology museum. It is a general science popularization facility that aims to implement a strategy of revitalizing the country through science and education and improving the nation's scientific and technological qualities. The first-stage of the project was completed and opened to the public on September 22, 1988. The second stage received visitors after completion on April 29, 2000.

The newly-opened China Science and Technology Museum, covering an area of 102,000 sq. m, is located near the Beijing Olympic Park. The new museum was completed in September 2009. The main form of education at the China Science and Technology Museum is through educational exhibits on scientific knowledge that includes scientific principles and technology applications. As well as conducting such exhibitions, the museum also organizes mass events and public lectures.

The Shanghai Science and Technology Museum is a large science popularization site funded and constructed by its local government. The Ninth

---
[2] With display space of length 10 m and above.

The China Science and Technology Museum opened in September 2009.

Asia-Pacific Economic Cooperation (APEC) Informal Leadership Meeting held in Shanghai in October 2001 was held at the Shanghai Science and Technology Museum.

The Haier Science and Technology Museum is China's first modern science and technology museum funded by an enterprise. It was launched in 1998 and officially received visitors in 1999. The large museum curates exhibitions related to corporate culture that integrates science and technology, culture, tourism, and entertainment.

Science Education Centers Taking advantage of existing resources for scientific and technological activities and opening them to the public is important for China's science and technology facilities. In 1996, the National Science and Technology Committee and the CAS decided on a number of science education pilot centers that would be opened to the public. These were the Institute of Physics, the Institute of Chemistry of the CAS, the Institute of Botany, the Institute of Vertebrate Paleontology, the Institute of Paleoanthropology, and the Computer Research Center.

Science Caravan and Science Train The CAST developed a "Science Caravan," which is also known as the Mobile Museum of Science and Technology, in line with the national popularization of science. The purpose of

The Shanghai Science and Technology Museum is located in Shanghai's Pudong New Area and is a landmark building along the Huangpu River.

A night view of the Museum of Chinese Wetlands in Hangzhou.

the Science Caravan is to spread scientific and technological knowledge, provide scientific and technological advice, and hold science exhibitions in remote and outlying areas of the country. The science caravan has five main functions:

- it has onboard exhibits on science and technology;
- it displays promotional panels related to science education;
- it offers scientific and technological films;
- it distributes books on science and technology popularization; and
- it is a mobile stage for science and technology popularization activities.

Launched in January 2001, the Science Caravan has carried out many science education activities in the vast western rural areas, that received a warm welcome from rural citizens. In 2007, the Science Center of CAST allotted a set of 52 mobile panels for the Exhibition of Science and Technology on Conserving Energy and Resources, Protecting the Eco-Environment, and Safeguarding Health and Security with the main theme being water resources. Based on regional features, local conditions, and audience customs, local institutes also carry out science caravan-like activities.

This picture shows the Science Caravan arriving in a village in Fanchang County, Anhui Province. Eager children brave the rain to take part in the activities organized by the Science Caravan.

In 2002, China rolled out the Science Train that traveled to the western regions of China but was also meant for the young and elderly people living in outlying and poor areas. The train's main mission was to organize science popularization activities such as exhibitions, seminars, lectures, clinics for agricultural technology advice, medical skills training sessions, entrepreneurship sharing sessions, screening of science-related films, and so on.

Science Popularization Media

The popularization of science and technology could not have been done without the support of the mass media. The findings of the Public Science Literacy Survey of China have shown the importance of the mass media in giving the public access to scientific and technological information. The Chinese mass media are also actively involved in science popularization.

Television   In China, television has become the most important channel for the public to acquire scientific and technological information. This has resulted in the broadcast of many science and technology popularization programs in the television networks. In 1997, the China Central Television set aside Channel 7 as an exclusive channel for popularizing science and technology to a rural audience. Channel 10 is a dedicated science channel, exclusively established for disseminating science and technology information. Besides these, there are also other science and technology popularization and science promotional programs on other channels. Local television stations have also set up channels or programs to popularize and promote science and technology. Many provincial television stations have established special science and technology programs and broadcasting departments have also set up regular science programs.

Newspapers   As the second largest channel for the Chinese public to obtain scientific and technological information, newspapers play an active role in science popularization. The first newspaper on science and technology, *Kexue Xiaobao* (*Science Compact News*), was founded in March 1954. Today, there are more than 60 science and technology newspapers such as *Keji Ribao* (*Science and Technology Daily*), and *Kexue Shibao* (*Contemporary Science*). Among these newspapers, some are funded by the central government or local governments, and some by scientific research units and mass organizations. They are distributed throughout the country. Mainstream newspapers such as *People's Daily*, *Guangming Daily*, and *Economics Daily* all have science and technology pages and columns, while *Science and Technology Daily* has a weekly column.

The Internet There are professional websites on science and technology issues, such as

- the *Zhongguo Kepu* (*China Science Popularization*) website (www.kepu.gov.cn) hosted by the Ministry of Science and Technology;
- the China Public Science and Technology Network (www.cpst.net.cn) founded by the China Association for Science and Technology; and
- the China Science and Technology Information Network (www.istic.ac.cn) under the China Science and Technology Information Institute.

Books and Magazines Apart from the three different types of mass media mentioned above, magazines and books also play an important role in the popularization of science. The Ministry of Science and Technology has allocated special funding to sponsor the Peking Union Medical College Press, the Chemical Industry Press, and the Beijing Institute of Technology Press to publish books related to popular science under the national science and technology program.

In 2006, a total of 3,162 popular science books were published throughout the country, with a total print run of 49 million. The number of science magazines reached 568, with 133 billion copies printed. The number of published science and technology newspapers reached 404 million copies. The total radio broadcast duration of science and technology programs throughout the country was 99,200 hours and those broadcast by television stations reached 113,800 hours. By the end of 2006, a total of 1,456 professional science and technology websites were built and funded by the central government.

In 2007, many excellent science and technology programs won national science and technology awards. A total of seven popular science works won the National Science and Technology Progress Award. Four were popular science books and the other three were audio-visual products. These included *Wuli Gaibian Shijie* (*Changes in the Physical World*), popular science comic novels such as *Zhaoqi Yonghu Shouche* (*Biogas Handbook)*, national defense science and technology documentary series such as *Shiji Bingge* (*Twenty-first-century Weapons)*, among others.

Achievements in Science Popularization

The Chinese government is working toward strengthening science popularization in various new ways. It has released a series of policies and plans on the development of science popularization, organized many influential science activities, and further improved science popularization facilities. All these have improved the public's knowledge of science and technology.

CHINESE CITIZEN'S SCIENCE LITERACY SURVEY

At the end of 2007, the CAST carried out the Seventh Spot Survey on Chinese Citizen's Science Literacy. The survey queried the public's level of understanding on scientific and technological issues, participation in science activities, and understanding of science and technology. The results showed a basic scientific literacy ratio of 2.25%, the highest among similar surveys done in the past.

Proportion of public participation and utilization of science popularization facilities (2005/2007)

Areas of Participation and Visits	2005	2007	Increase (%)
Participation in activities			
Science and technology training	30.8	35.2	4.4
Science and technology consultation	30.4	32.4	2.0
Science and technology lectures	23.9	25.8	1.9
Science and Technology Week	11.9	14.7	2.8
Science Caravan activities	11.6	13.8	2.2
Visits to centers and infrastructures			
Zoos, aquariums, and botanical gardens	30.3	51.9	21.6
Science popularization galleries and model displays	36.7	46.8	10.1
Reading rooms	29.2	43.7	14.5
Public libraries	26.7	41.0	14.3
Science and technology demonstrations and science popularization activity stations	30.9	29.1	−1.8
Art galleries of museums	11.2	17.5	6.3
Science and technology centers	9.3	16.7	7.4
Natural science museums	7.1	13.9	6.8

Source: China Association of Science and Technology.

The results of the 2007 Spot Survey on Chinese Citizen's Science Literacy showed an increase in the number of citizens participating in science activities. Compared with the 2005 official statistics, there were increases in the ratios of public participation in science activities, utilization, and visits of various science popularization facilities and infrastructure. Numbers were especially high in the activities of visiting zoos, aquariums, or botanical gardens, and science galleries, as well as the use of reading rooms and public libraries.

Science Activities

Large-scale science popularization activities in China include the science and technology week, major science exhibitions, campaigns to bring science and technology to rural villages, and so on.

Science and Technology Week

The Science and Technology Week is an important science popularization activity and one that is rich in content. All organizations involved in science and technology activities nationwide actively participate in the popularization of science and technology and encourage the public to learn more about contemporary science. Every year, the National Science and Technology Popularization Joint Conference selects a theme for the Science and Technology Week, and related departments carry out various science activities based on the theme.

Themes of previous science and technology weeks have included

- Science and Technology: Creating the Future (2002);
- Depending on Science and Technology to Defeat SARS (2003);
- Science and Technology: Tools for Building A Prosperous Society (2004–2005); and
- Building an Innovative Country Together (2006–2009).

During the Science and Technology Week of 2009, scientific and technological personnel visited enterprises and rural and grassroots areas to popularize science and technology, promote the spirit of innovation, and provide information to the public. These activities brought scientific and technological results to the transformation and upgrading of enterprises and boosted local economic development. The primary task of current scientific and technological efforts is for the nation to use it to cope with the international financial crisis and promote a stable and rapid development of the economy. This will also be the theme of 2010's Science and Technology Week.

ORIGIN OF SCIENCE AND TECHNOLOGY WEEK

Science and Technology Week was launched in 2001. It won approval from the State Council and the Ministry of Science and Technology. Together with other relevant departments, Science and Technology Week is held in the third week of May every year. The first was themed "Science and Technology is around me," and its events were carried out in provinces and cities nationwide.

Early in 1987, the city of Hangzhou held a Science and Technology Promotion Week. In the summer of the same year, Shanghai organized the month-long Summer of Science and Technology that is now held every year. Since 1991, it has been renamed as the Shanghai Science and Technology Festival. Making use of the non-farming season, Heilongjiang Province and Jilin Province organized the Winter of Science and Technology to launch science popularization activities in rural areas. This activity has spread to over 10 municipalities, provinces, and autonomous regions in the north.

As the most popular public science and technology event, and one that covers the largest area and exerts the most influences, the activities of the Science and Technology Week arouse much public interest. Although both initiatives only last for a short period of time, they still manage to create enthusiasm among scientific and technological personnel to promote science, increase awareness and the understanding of science and technology among the public and most of all, to deepen the social effects of science and technology.

Science Lectures, Exhibitions, and Contests

Leveraging on major international and domestic festivals, related science popularization units actively carry out various science popularization activities. For example, during International Meteorological Day, World Health Day, World Environment Day, World Earth Day, International Museum Day, National Arbor Day, and National Energy Conservation Awareness Week,

Attendance of science lectures and exhibitions held by the CAST system (2007)

Item	Number of science lectures held	Number of attendees for lectures (10,000 persons)	Number of science exhibitions organized	Visitors to galleries and exhibitions (10,000 persons)	Number of programs on the mass media
Associations at county-level	81,417	4,181.54	36,479	6,615.43	48,156
Local associations	27,930	801.69	10,997	2,373.7	16,009
Provincial associations	2,462	1201.02	1,388	805.24	1,068
CAST	133	10.46	18	65.23	11
CAST subtotal	111,672	6,194.71	48,882	9,859.6	65,244
Total	**142,455**	**7,087.65**	**53,246**	**10,882.89**	**73,958**

Source: *China Association of Science and Technology.*

During the National Science and Technology Week and Shanghai Science and Technology Festival, three generations of a family interact with an insect model.

these units propagate corresponding scientific knowledge based on their local situations. They undertake promotional efforts through the mass media such as newspapers, radio stations, television stations and the Internet, as well as through science competitions, lectures, and cultural performances.

Science popularization activities targeting rural areas place special emphasis on the spread of practical techniques. Since 1996, local organizations have launched cultural, science, and health activities in rural areas during winter and spring. More than 100 million scientific and technological personnel have visited rural areas to help improve the cultural and scientific knowledge of these citizens. One of the activities organized include science lectures, and it is estimated that in 2002 alone, CAST and its affiliated organizations held 90,000 science lectures that attracted more than three million participants.

Science Activities for Youths

To promote scientific literacy comprehensively, the State Council promulgated the National Action Plan for Scientific Literacy in 2006. This plan called for substantial improvements in the national scientific literacy of citizens through education and the spread and popularization of science and technology. Young students were the major targets for this initiative. Based on the progress of primary and secondary school reforms, various social resources have been set up to provide young students with science popularization sites through different channels in various forms.

All Chinese primary and secondary schools have educational resources to fully implement high-quality education plans during their education reforms. They also improved the use of science in basic education and promoted the implementation of new science curricula. They explored an innovative model for science and technology education and strengthened the construction of scientific and technological facilities in the schools. Various science popularization activities were organized through activity groups and clubs. They also developed effective approaches and methods, which linked social science activities with science curricula. Thus, modes, forms, and contents of social science activities were enriched. For example, they organized primary and secondary school student visits to key national laboratories to enhance the educational value of social science activities.

The country supports and organizes various contests that are beneficial to the development of youth's scientific literacy and innovation skills. A series of influential activities, such as the National Youth Science and Technology Invention Contest, the International Academic Olympics for Secondary Schools, the National Challenge Trophy for Undergraduates'

This picture shows students from Beijing's Bayi Middle School installing a simple telephone during the Happy Science on Campus program.

Extra-Curricular Academic Science and Technology Competition, "Big Hands Hold Little Hands"—A Movement for Youth Science and Technology Communication, "Youths' Visit to the World of Science," "Our Future Engineers"—A Design and Skills Competition, and the China Youth Computer Robot Contest.

With strong support from local scientific research institutes, local youth leagues and youth pioneers organizations have taken advantage of these activities and contests to carry out various science education programs with remarkable results. From 2005 to 2006, CAST held about 20,000 youth science and technology contests that attracted more than 60 million contestants. It organized over 7,200 youth science and technology summer and winter camps, attended by 1.4 million youths. In 2007, CAST, the Ministry of Education, the Central Committee of the Communist Youth League, the CCCPC Office of Capital Spiritual Civilization Construction Commission and the State Administration of Radio, Film, and Television jointly launched the "Water by My Side—Youth Scientific Investigations Program." Around 300,000 young people took part in the hometown survey of water resources and water experiments, and 150,000 handed in their results and put forward 15,000 pieces of advice on how to conserve water.

Universities and Scientific Research Institutes' Opening up to the Public

A key part of the construction of an innovative country is the continual improvement of national scientific literacy. To strengthen the openness and sharing of science education resources, establish a close relationship between science and technology personnel and the public, and also inspiring the public, especially the youth's interest in science and technology, the Ministry of Science and Technology, the Propaganda Department of the CCCPC, the National Reform and Development Commission, the Ministry of Education, the Ministry of Finance, CAST and CAS jointly released the Decision on Scientific Research Institutes and Universities Opening up to the Public for Science Popularization Activities.

This decision required scientific research institutes and universities to open up their premises for public visits. The institutions also have to organize science activities by making use of their scientific research facilities and sites so as to benefit the public. It also states that the institutions should help improve China's science education and enhance the public's innovation awareness, create a encouraging atmosphere of innovation and improve the public's scientific literacy. They also need to train future science and technology personnel to accelerate scientific and technological development and enhance independent innovation.

Scientific research institutes and universities that are open to the public include research units that work on natural sciences, engineering and technology, and other related universities. These institutions are built and sponsored by governments at all levels. The projects opened to the public are research and experiment centers, such as laboratories, engineering

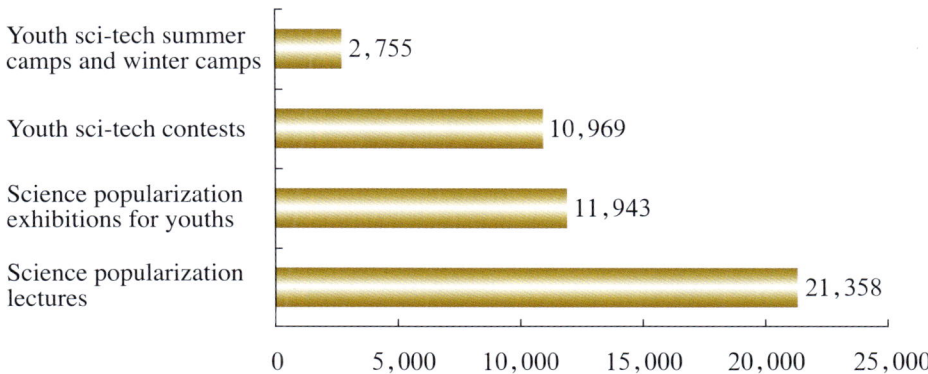

Source: *China Statistical Yearbook (2008)*

Youth science activities held by CAST (2007)

centers, technical centers, and field stations of scientific research institutes and universities. Scientific research infrastructure such as instrument centers, analysis and testing centers, natural sciences and technology resources libraries, science data centers and networks, scientific and technological literature centers, and scientific and technological information service centers or networks are within the scope of this program. Unclassified scientific research instruments and facilities and experiment and observation sites, science and technology museums, herbariums, galleries, astronomical observatories, museums, and botanical gardens are also included.

Scientific research institutes and universities should adhere to the principle of opening up to the public not for profit but for highlighting social benefits. These opening-up activities fully demonstrate their efforts to be practical, experimental, participatory, and effective. Institutes and universities hold activities to attract audiences to observe scientific research, participate in scientific research practice, and to discuss scientific and technological problems. Such activities increase the audience's interest in and understanding of science and technology. They also enhance their ability to solve problems through scientific and technological means.

The goals for promoting the opening-up to the public in the 11th Five-Year Plan period included opening affiliated scientific research institutes of the

This picture shows an open house session conducted by the Chinese Academy of Sciences, where the public interacted with the academicians.

CAS, social non-profit scientific research institutes under the State Council, and related universities of the Project 211 before the end of 2008. By the end of 2010, scientific research institutes and universities affiliated to other ministries, departments, and local governments aim to learn from the experience of such activities carried out by institutions that had opened up to the public. Official statistics show that in 2009, affiliated scientific research institutes of the CAS and universities directly under the Ministry of Education had opened 430 sites to the public and more than 7 million people participated in activities that played an important role in helping people understand, explore, and experience science.

International Exchanges for Science Popularization

International exchanges for science popularization refers to activities such as receptions, appointments to attend meetings, visits, exhibitions, and training that concern science popularization between related departments and units of China and other countries and regions. In recent years, international exchanges and cooperation for science popularization in China have generally improved and the number of participants has increased rapidly. In 2006, a total of 2,132 international exchange activities linked to science popularization were held that attracted 656,500 participants.

APEC Youth Science Festival The Third APEC Youth Science Festival was held in Beijing during August 3–9, 2004. Its theme was "Science, Youth, and the Future." This festival was the first large-scale APEC activity held in China and combined the themes of science and youth. It was jointly sponsored by the Ministry of Science and Technology, the Ministry of Education, CAST, the Central Committee of the Communist Youth League, and the Beijing Municipal Government. It received support from the Ministry of Foreign Affairs, the Ministry of Finance, the CAS, the Chinese Academy of Engineering, and the Commission of National Natural Science Foundation of China.

Fourteen out of the 21 member economies of APEC (with Macau as an APEC observer) sent delegations. The number of participants in the festival reached 1,200. Of this number, more than 800 were Chinese delegates, while the remaining 400 came from other member or observer economies. The number of exhibition booths in the science exhibition was 200, and the exhibition area covered 6,000 sq. m.

As an international event, APEC Youth Science Festival showed China's efforts in scientific literacy education and also improved understanding and friendship between youths in the Asia-Pacific region by promoting mutual learning and exchanges. It encouraged Chinese students to face future challenges, build scientific literacy that matched the current needs of the world, and

This picture, taken on October 15, 2009, shows the opening ceremony of the 13th Meeting of the China–U.S. Joint Commission on Scientific and Technological Cooperation, held in Washington D.C. Left to right: Zhou Wenzhong, Chinese ambassador to the United States; Wan Gang, Minister of Science and Technology of China; John Holdren, Director of the White House Office of Science and Technology Policy; Kerri-Ann Jones, U.S. Assistant Secretary of State for Oceans and International Environmental and Scientific Affairs; and Ralph Cicerone, President of the U.S. National Academy of Sciences.

fostered an aspiration of actively participating in global science and technology competitions. Through this festival, the Chinese government advocated the scientific spirit and the learning, studying, and popularizing of science to teach youths to adopt a scientific outlook on the world and life in general. It reflects the heritage of China's ancient culture and a continuation of the creative scientific spirit for member economies.

China-U.S. Young Scientific and Technological Personnel Exchange Program During the 10th Meeting of the China–U.S. Joint Commission on Scientific and Technological Cooperation held in April 2002, the Ministry of Science and Technology signed the China–U.S. Young Scientific and Technological Personnel Exchange Program with the U.S. National Science Foundation. The goal of the program was to send American postgraduates to universities, research institutes, and laboratories in China to conduct research with China's young researchers over eight weeks. This program aims to encourage exchange and cooperation between young scholars of the two countries and to promote mutual understanding and friendship, as well as to train both countries' personnel and lay the foundation for future scientific and technological cooperation between China and the United States.

From 2004 to 2007, the program sent around 30 outstanding American postgraduates to participate in research activities in China every year. While earning research experience in China, American students also acquired knowledge of China's science and technology, political and economic systems, foreign policy, history, culture and education, and social customs. In related institutes of the CAS and laboratories of China's top universities, opinions were exchanged with Chinese science and technology personnel. Both parties explored and discussed each other's working methods and scientific research management systems, and together tackled problems encountered in scientific research. All these had a significant impact on scientific cooperation between the two countries.

Chapter 6

....

International Cooperation on Science, Technology, and Education

C hina's efforts on international cooperation in science, technology, and education are closely linked to the country's economic, technological, and diplomatic strategies. To drive reforms and innovation, China adheres to the "basic position of focusing on the improvement of the innovation capability of China that serves the two key issues of modernizing socialist principles and the country's diplomacy." It also looks at expanding minds and conducting pioneering and innovative work to drive progress in her bilateral and multilateral science, technology, and education cooperation.

Intergovernmental Science and Technology Cooperation

By the end of 2007, China had signed 102 inter-governmental science and technology cooperation agreements and intergovernmental economics and technology cooperation agreements, and more than 1,000 interdepartmental science and technology cooperation agreements with 96 countries around the world. A complete bilateral and multilateral intergovernmental international framework in science and technology cooperation was thus shaped. From 2007, some developed countries launched initiatives to jointly provide support for R&D cooperation in priority areas. According to official statistics, the total funding for science and technology cooperation with China reached RMB 700 million.

China–U.S. Science and Technology Cooperation

The related departments of the Chinese and the U.S. governments have signed more than 50 cooperation protocols or memorandums under the framework of the China–U.S. Scientific and Technological Cooperation Agreement. The two countries have carried out fruitful cooperation in basic research and research in the areas of energy, resources, environment, agriculture, and sanitation. This cooperation created a good relationship between governments, scientific research institutes, and enterprises, and exchanges between science and technology personnel have progressed smoothly.

The Second China–U.S. Strategic Economic Dialogue was held in Washington D.C. in May 2007. Both China and the United States passed the Principle and Achievements of Strengthening Innovation Cooperation within the Strategic Economic Framework, and signed the Sino–U.S. Memorandum of Cooperation on Nuclear Safety AP 1000 Reactor. The China–U.S. Innovation Conference was held in Beijing in December 2007 as an important follow-up activity. During the conference, China and the United States discussed cooperation on innovation.

Outcome of Key Science and Technology Cooperation In October 2007, the Daya Bay Reactor Neutrino Experiment was launched in the Shenzhen Daya Bay Nuclear Power Base. It was the largest cooperation effort between China and the United States in the area of basic research. A total of 34 research units from six countries, including China, the United States, and Russia, participated in the Daya Bay Reactor Neutrino Experiment International Cooperation Group. To date, the project design and demonstration, detector design and key small model test have been successfully completed. The project is now sufficiently mature to move into the equipment manufacturing stage.

New Progress in Industrial Science and Technology Cooperation Under the active promotion of the Ministry of Science and Technology and other ministries, the China Huaneng Group joined the United States' nonprofit FutureGen Alliance. It participated in international cooperation and kept track of and mastered frontier technologies on clean energy development. Concurrently, the GreenGen Program proposed by Huaneng Group created a new alliance with the U.S. Peabody Energy Corporation in December 2007. This marked a significant step forward in international cooperation. In addition, China launched the R&D Cooperation of Magnesium Alloy Body with the U.S. Department of Energy and Canada's Natural Resources.

China–European Union Science and Technology Cooperation

The European Union (EU) and its member countries are important partners of China in international science and technology cooperation. According to the People's Republic of China and the European Community Scientific and Technological Cooperation Agreement signed in 1998, the EU Framework Program became the first foreign science and technology program that was open to China.

China–EU Science and Technology Year   In November 2006, the Ministry of Science and Technology and the European Commission Directorate-General for Research jointly organized the China–EU Science and Technology Year. The China–EU Science and Technology Year is an important result of the high-level strategic cooperation in science and technology between China and the EU in recent years. It has created favorable conditions for both sides to achieve comprehensive and in-depth cooperation. In the first year, China and the EU organized 40 exhibitions, forums, symposiums, and held follow-up energy seminars, a China–EU Chinese Medicine Conference and the first China–EU Robotics Workshop.

This picture, taken on May 12, 2005, shows the China–EU High-Level Forum on Science and Technology Strategy jointly sponsored by the Chinese Ministry of Science and Technology, the EU Directorate-General for Research, and the EU President, the Grand Duchy of Luxembourg. It was held in the Great Hall of the People in Beijing and more than 400 science and technology officials, renowned scholars, and entrepreneurs from China and the EU presented at the forum.

China–EU Science and Technology Partnership Program In the Sixth China–EU Science and Technology Cooperation Steering Committee Meeting held in November 2007, China and the EU unanimously agreed to build a reciprocal cooperation mechanism, and thus initiated the China–EU Science and Technology Partnership Program, in which China and the EU jointly decided on strategic priority areas and also agreed that both parties would jointly collect, evaluate, and determine partnership programs and respectively invest no less than 30 million in the joint projects.

Other Important Cooperations Through cooperation under the China–EU Framework Program, China and the EU developed a 2.5G high-speed Internet backbone, which has greatly improved information and scientific data exchanges between China and the EU. The Sino–Germany Joint Laser Laboratory is progressing smoothly. Advanced laser equipment provided by Germany is already in place. Cooperation between China and the United Kingdom in dry pulverized coal gasification technology has generated the first round of data on the high temperatures and the pressure gas reaction of Chinese coal.

China–Russia Science and Technology Cooperation

Under the China–Russia Premiers Regular Meeting Committee, there is a special science and technology cooperation subcommittee. The subcommittee is responsible for coordinating and managing science and technology cooperation between China and Russia.

Russia Year In 2006, China held a "Russia Year," whereby both countries jointly carried out 21 scientific and technological activities such as a seminar series, the High-level Forum on Sino–Russia Science and Technology Cooperation, the Russia Science and Technology Exhibition and Project Matchmaking Symposium, the China–Russia Science and Technology Cultural Exchange, and the inauguration of the Veteran and Middle-aged Scientists Association.

After the success of the first "Russia Year," both countries held a "China Year" in Russia in 2007, in which they co-organized 25 science and technology activities, including science and technology exhibitions, a series of high-level symposiums, scientific and technological cooperation forums, and a sizeable number of science and technology introductions and matchmaking meetings.

Sino–Russia Science and Technology Park The Yantai China–Russia High-Tech Industrialization Cooperation Demonstration Base, the

This picture shows Chinese and Russian forestry experts exchanging views on cultivation techniques in the China–Russia Science and Technology Cooperation Park at the Heihe City's Forestry Bureau.

Heilongjiang China–Russia Scientific and Technological Cooperation and Industrialization Center, and the Zhejiang China–Russia Science and Technology Park have made substantial progress. After three years of exploration and development, the China–Russia Moscow Friendship Science and Technology Park has become more influential and is playing a more important role in boosting scientific and technological innovation cooperation between China and Russia.

Significant Advances in Relations   The key China–Russia scientific and technological cooperation projects, the No. 1 and No. 2 units of the Tianwan Nuclear Power Plant, located in Lianyungang City, Jiangsu Province, entered commercial operation in 2007. This plant is the largest technological and economic cooperation project between China and Russia by far, and is also China's largest installed capacity nuclear power plant. Through cooperation with Russia, the first manned submersible capable of diving to ocean depths of 7,000 m was developed and produced by China. It underwent submarine diving tests in November 2007.

Cooperation with Other Countries

Through the joint efforts of China, Japan, and the Republic of Korea (ROK), the First China–Japan–ROK Science and Technology Ministers' Meeting was held in January 2007 in the Republic of Korea, marking a new phase in scientific and technological cooperation among these three countries. Since then, the China, Japan, and ROK Science and Technology Ministers' Meeting and the China-Japan-ROK Scientific and Technological Cooperation Secretaries' Meeting have co-existed to promote more effective scientific and technological cooperation among the three countries through policy exchanges and concrete implementation.

China has also carried out scientific and technological cooperation in many areas with African countries, Canada, Singapore, New Zealand, Australia, Mongolia, Brazil, Argentina, and Israel. In addition, China has achieved remarkable results in cooperation with East European countries and countries of the Commonwealth of Independent States in areas of microelectronics, optical technology, laser technology, mechanical manufacturing, information technology, biotechnology, medicine, and sustainable agriculture.

Studies Abroad and the Teaching of Chinese as a Foreign Language

Studying Abroad

Studying in China Foreign students have long been an important component of China's education system. In 1950, China only received 33 foreign students from Eastern Europe. but in 2008, she received 1.46 million international students. Since the reform and opening up three decades ago, China has witnessed a rapid increase in her efforts to attract foreign students. In 2008, a total of 223,499 foreign students from 189 countries and regions came to China, studying in 592 institutions of higher learning, scientific research institutes, and other teaching institutions.

Foreign students from Asia made up the largest group, accounting for 152,931 students or 68.43% of the total for the year. The number of students from Africa and Oceania increased significantly, with year-on-year growth of 48.76% and 45.68%, respectively. Divided according to each country, the top three originating countries for students were South Korea (66,806), the United States (19,914), and Japan (16,733). To further improve the quality of foreign

The 80,000-square-meter ASy Scintillator Detector Array co-developed by China and Japan, is located in the Tibet Yangbajing Universe Observatory compound, 90 km northwest of Lhasa. The observatory is not only China's largest geothermal energy base, but also the highest observatory in the northern hemisphere.

students, the Ministry of Education reformed the Chinese Government Scholarship Students Admissions in 2008. This reform allocated some of the Chinese Government Scholarship funds to border provinces and universities for their own recruitment and to encourage these provinces and universities to attract postgraduate students with masters degrees and above.

Chinese Students Studying Abroad Since the reform and opening up, China's efforts to send her students for oversea studies have gone from start-up to development, and thence to continuous improvement. Studying abroad has become an important window of China's reform and opening-up process as well as a source of foreign exchange. A foreign study management and operation system that is compatible with social and economic development has gradually moved from the central government to local governments, and from institutions of higher learning to scientific research institutions.

Three major channels for foreign study—studying abroad with national funds, unit funds, or at one's own expense—have taken shape. These channels have complementary advantages and play different roles. From 1978 to the end of 2008, the number of students abroad was 1,315,000, of which 389,100 have returned.

This picture, taken on June 28, 2005, shows the Polish student Pawel Matuewicz chatting with a classmate from Benin at the Beijing Language and Culture University 2005 Session Graduate Ceremony. Pawel was the most eye-catching student in that ceremony. He studied at the Beijing Language and Culture University for 10 years and obtained his bachelor, masters, and doctorate degrees, becoming the first western foreign student to earn three consecutive degrees in China.

To date, 1,002,400 Chinese people are studying abroad. Of these, 735,400 are currently working on bachelors or masters degrees, or doctorates, and carrying out post-doctoral research or academic visits. A comparison of official statistics from 2007 and 2008 shows that, the number of students abroad and the number of returning students have both increased. The number of students abroad went up by 35,200, 24.43%, and that of returned students rose by 24,900, an increase of 55.95%.

Returning students play a significant role in areas of education, scientific research, high-tech industry, finance, insurance, trade, and management. They are an important force in China's national economic and social development. At the same time, efforts to serve the country through appropriate means are increasingly vigorous. Students who are studying abroad serve the country by way of short-term returning lecturers, academic exchanges, scientific research cooperation, program and funding, and providing information and technical advisory services. In recent years, local governments, enterprises, and units have drawn up and issued a series of policy provisions designed to support and attract students who study abroad to return and work in their homeland or serve China in other appropriate ways.

These provisions have built and improved the relevant management and service agencies and a talent pool of overseas students. There are also many kinds of special funds set up for overseas students.

Teaching of Chinese as a Foreign Language

In order to promote Chinese culture, the Chinese government established the National Leading Group for Teaching Chinese as a Foreign Language (known as Hanban) in 1987. The leading group aims to promote the Chinese language to the world, spread awareness of Chinese culture, promote a global understanding and friendship toward China, and boost world peace and development.

Chinese Bridge   In 2004, the State Council approved the Teaching of Chinese to Foreigners Development Plan 2003–2007, known as the Chinese Bridge, drawn up by the National Leading Group for Teaching Chinese as a Foreign Language.

A key step forward was to establish the Headquarters of the Confucius Institute in Beijing and set up branches in countries around the world. Teaching of the Chinese language in foreign countries was to be actively promoted and supported, and those countries involved were to be provided with Chinese language teaching resources.

China and the United States jointly researched and developed online Chinese teaching courseware for primary and secondary school students. The courseware brings Chinese to the classrooms, develops students' interest in learning Chinese, and changes their concept that "Chinese is hard to learn." It also takes advantage of modern teaching technology, creates new teaching models, and carries out multi-party cooperation to create good teaching materials. It has built up a team of high-level Chinese teaching staff and nurtured a number of Chinese teachers who have mastered modern distance education technology and multimedia language teaching theory and methods. It has picked 10 high-quality universities as a form of advisory board for Chinese language teaching. It has also reformed and improved *Hanyu Shuiping Kaoshi* (HSK)[1] to maintain its international branding and enable it to realize the scale and level of renowned international examinations. The group also holds a World Chinese Conference and Chinese Bridge Competition, and works to attract more foreign young people to learn Chinese. It has set up the Chinese Bridge Fund, which is used to carry out various Chinese language-related activities in foreign countries.

---

[1] Chinese proficiency test for non-native speakers.

This picture, taken on July 16, 2009, shows the opening ceremony of the Eighth Chinese Bridge Chinese Proficiency Competition for Foreign College Students. It was jointly sponsored by the National Chinese International Promotion Leading Group Office and the Hunan Provincial Government and was held in Changsha City, Hunan Province.

Confucius Institute   The Confucius Institute is not a college in the usual sense. Instead, it is an institute for spreading Chinese culture and cultural exchanges and is regarded as a non-profit social welfare institution. One of the most important functions of the Confucius Institute is to provide standard and authoritative modern Chinese textbooks for Chinese learners around the world and to provide a formal and important channel for Chinese language teaching.

The headquarters of the Confucius Institute is in Beijing and was set up in 2007. Confucius institutes outside China are its affiliates, founded through cooperation between China and foreign countries. Confucius is a "mascot" of traditional Chinese culture. Therefore, choosing Confucius as the brand name for Chinese language teaching is a sign of the revival of traditional Chinese culture.

The first Confucius Institute was set up in Seoul, South Korea, on November 21, 2004. By August 2009, there were 268 Confucius institutes and 71 Confucius classrooms in 83 countries and regions all over the world. A total of 61 domestic colleges, universities, and institutes have taken part in cooperative teaching at the Confucius Institute. These mainly send teachers abroad and also recruit volunteers. By 2010, there will be 500 Confucius institutes and classrooms located around the world.

This picture, taken on May 30, 2007, shows the Confucius Institute co-established by the China Zhejiang Normal University and the Ukraine Lugansk Normal University. It was the first Confucius Institute founded in Ukraine by China.

Other Programs Hanban was initially set up as the AP Chinese Project with the United States College Board in 2003 to promote Chinese in the United States. In April 2006, the two parties signed a formal agreement to cooperate in a series of Chinese language and cultural projects. The National Office for Teaching Chinese as a Foreign Language (NOCFL) organizes the World Youth Student Summer Camp and invites youths from around the world to China to attend the three-week summer camp. This camp aims to improve exchanges between Chinese and foreign youths, deepen their understanding and personal experience of Chinese language and culture, and stimulate their enthusiasm for learning Chinese.

The NOCFL also organizes visits to China for delegations composed of principals of primary and secondary schools from other countries, and invites principals of primary and secondary schools and education officials from the United States, United Kingdom, and South Korea to attend a one-week visit to China. The goal of these visits is to deepen their understanding of Chinese language and culture, to persuade schools in foreign countries to conduct Chinese language courses, to build up an exchange platform for Chinese and foreign schools, and to carry out Chinese teaching cooperation.

British middle school students took part in the Chinese Summer Camp at Xiamen, during which they visited the homes of Xiamen middle school students.

Technology Trade and International Intellectual Property Protection

Technology Market and Trade

Technology trade is an important part of China's market system and a bridge that links scientific research and production, as well as being a factor of the market system.

In 2007, the total imports and exports of China's high-tech production reached US$634.8 billion, with US$347.82 billion of exports and US$286.98 billion of imports. The momentum of high-tech products propelled a further optimization of the overall structure of China's merchandise trade. Exports and imports of high-tech products took up 28.6% and 30%, respectively, of total merchandise exports and imports.

In 2007, there were 220,900 registered technology contracts, with a total turnover of RMB 222.65 billion. Technology development, technology transfer, technology advisory bodies, and technology services all increased. The total turnover of technology development contracts reached RMB 87.6 billion, accounting for 39.4%, and occupied the top position for the four types of contracts. Technology transfer activities were also more active. The total turnover was RMB 42 billion, which was 19% of the total turnover for the entire country. The respective turnovers for technology services and technology advisory bodies were RMB 84 billion and RMB 9 billion, with a year-on-year increase of 20.9% and 5.9%, respectively.

As enterprises become more aware of intellectual property protection and its utilization have been strengthened, an increasing number of technologies involved in intellectual property have been transferred and converted through the technology market.

In 2007, out of all the traded contracts in the national technology market, a total of 109,740 involved intellectual property, including technology secrets, computer software, patents, integrated circuits, biomedical products, and new hybrid varieties of flora and fauna. These accounted for 49.7% of total traded contracts. Turnover was RMB 147.7 billion or 66.4% of the total turnover. The turnover for technology secrets and computer software copyrights ranked first and second, at RMB 100.8 billion and RMB 25.5 billion, respectively.

Enterprises remained as the largest producer and captive sector in technology trade, taking first place among all participants in the technology trade. In 2006, technology transactions from enterprises surpassed technology absorption transactions in terms of value for the first time. The output from technology transactions among enterprises reached new heights. In 2007, the number of technology contracts from enterprises hit 135,900 with a turnover

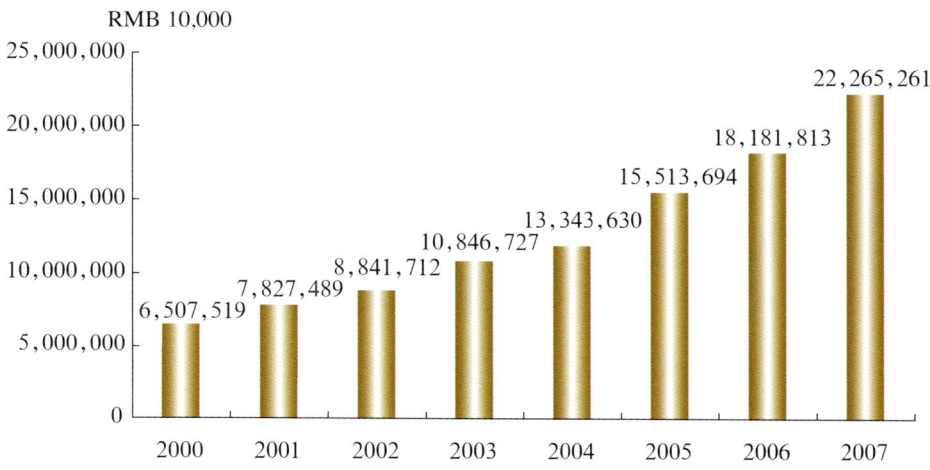

Source: *China Statistical Yearbook (2008)*

Turnover of China's technology market (2000–2007)

of RMB 192.3 billion, which accounted for 86.4% of the national turnover. Enterprises bought 169,300 pieces of technology. The traded technology turnover reached RMB 182.9 billion and took up 82.2% of the total national turnover.

Patent Applications

In 2007, PCT (Patent Cooperation Treaty) applications around the world hit a new record. China was ranked in the top 10 for the first time in 2005, and achieved rapid progress in subsequent years. In 2007, China had 5,456 patent applications, surpassing the Netherlands and reaching the world ranking of seventh place. The applications increased by 38.1% over the previous year and was the highest among the top 15 countries in the world in terms of PCT international applications. This increase not only reflected the rapid rise of China's innovation capability and growing awareness of protecting intellectual property, but also made great contributions to global intellectual property system reform.

The State Intellectual Property Office of China began to accept electronic applications formally from May 1, 2007. The total number of PCT-SAFE (Secure Applications Filed Electronically) applications in that year was 1,496, accounting for 27.4% of the total application volume. The use of PCT-SAFE not only provides patent applicants with a standard model for applications but also reduces their cost and facilitates the easy submission of application forms.

High-tech enterprises such as Huawei Technologies and ZTE Corporation have performed outstandingly in terms of PCT applications, and have contributed greatly to China's growing number of patent applications. In terms of PCT applications' global ranking, Huawei ranks fourth and ZTE is 53rd. Chinese enterprises aim to invest in overseas markets and pay greater attention to international intellectual property protection, investing large amounts in R&D and strengthening cooperation with foreign countries so as to benefit from these patents.

FYI
FOR YOUR
INFORMATION

ABOUT THE PCT

The Patent Cooperation Treaty (PCT) was signed in 1970 and came into effect in 1978. China joined the PCT on January 1, 1994, as a full member. Meanwhile, the Patent Office of China became an international receiving office, prosecution bureau, and primary inspection bureau for the PCT.

This picture, taken on December 4, 2006, shows the Sixth China-Japan-ROK Intellectual Property Office Directors Policy Dialogue held in Beijing. The three parties approved two new cooperation projects: statistical data exchange and Internet service assessment. They also reached a consensus on mid-term objectives for cooperation among their respective intellectual property offices. From left to right: Tian Lipu, Director of the State Intellectual Property Office of the People's Republic of China; Makoto Nakajima, Director of the Japan Patent Office; and Jun Sang-woo, Director of the South Korea Patent Office.

The Fight against Piracy

On April 26, 2008, which is also the World Intellectual Property Day, the National Office of Anti-Pornography and Anti-Illegal Publications encouraged local departments to investigate, resolve, and expose a number of key piracy cases. The office disseminated public warnings on intellectual property protection and the fight against piracy. It mobilized 31 provinces to carry out the 2008 National Destruction Activity of Pirated and Illegal Publications. During this campaign, 47.18 million pirated and illegal publications were destroyed, the largest amount ever destroyed at any one time.

The Press and Publication Administration, the National Copyright Administration, and the National Office of Anti-Pornography and Anti-Illegal Publications actively undertook efforts to prevent and combat piracy, and distributed audio-visual products on related topics during the Beijing 2008 Olympics Games' Opening and Closing Ceremonies.

During the 2008 Beijing Olympics, the National Copyright Administration worked with the Olympic Anti-Piracy Working Group established by the Beijing Organization Commission of the Olympic Games and the National Office of Anti-Pornography and Anti-Illegal Publications to strengthen supervision of network broadcast piracy. The working group worked for 24 hours every day and dealt with 117 infringing websites. They closed and stopped access to 84 websites, and took enforcement measures to order 33 websites to remove content or stop infringing copyright. The fastest case they handled took only 20 minutes to investigate and regulate, and involved a website that had illegally broadcast the Olympic Games. The reinforcement group's work received high praise from the International Olympic Committee, commended as demonstrating high standards in anti-piracy work.

Significant International Scientific Projects for China as Leader and Participant

In recent years, China has made major breakthroughs in some leading-edge international science and engineering programs in which it has participated and led. These achievements have played a significant role in improving China's ability to participate and compete in global scientific and technological cooperation. It has also enhanced its international influence and contributed to the scientific and technological development of the world.

TCM International Science and Technology Cooperation Program

In July 2006, the Ministry of Science and Technology, together with Ministry of Health and the State Administration of Traditional Chinese Medicine (TCM) issued and formally launched the TCM International Science and Technology Cooperation Plan and its program. This was the first major international science and engineering research program advocated and promulgated by the Chinese government.

The program aims to play a leading role in shifting the world's medical and health model, to support the construction of a harmonious society and the improvement of human health with the aid of science and technology. It has worked to develop international TCM science and technology cooperation platforms, made use of global science and technology resources, and taken on the treatment and prevention of major worldwide diseases that threaten human health as the basic starting point.

The TCM International Science and Technology Cooperation Program entered the implementation stage in 2007. In June, the Ministry of Science and Technology successfully held the China–EU TCM International Science and Technology Cooperation Conference in Europe. More than 400 delegates from China and 18 European countries attended the conference and identified five areas for potential cooperation.

In November 2007, the TCM International Science and Technology Cooperation Conference was held in Beijing and approximately 500 delegates from 41 countries, regions, and international organizations took part. Delegates jointly issued the Beijing Declaration on TCM International Science and Technology Cooperation. They achieved consensus on the inter-governmental promotion of wider TCM science and technology cooperation and the Preparatory Committee of the TCM International Science and Technology Cooperation Committee of Experts.

The two conferences have served to strengthen the consensus of foreign countries on carrying out international TCM science and technology cooperation and laying a foundation for substantive cooperation.

International Science and Technology Cooperation Program on Renewable Energy and New Energy

In November 2007, the Ministry of Science and Technology and the National Development and Reform Commission officially launched the International Science and Technology Cooperation Program on Renewable Energy and New Energy. The program prioritizes five aspects:

- the integration of solar power and solar-powered buildings,
- biomass fuels and biomass power,
- wind power,
- hydrogen and fuel cells, and
- natural gas hydrate development.

In addition, combined with bilateral science and technology cooperation, China launched a number of substantial international cooperation projects in the areas of renewable and new energy. For example, it launched large-scale cooperation projects on renewable energy with Italy in 2007, which included the Sichuan Maple Tree Bio-diesel Development and Industrialization Demonstration and the Shanghai Chongming Island One Megawatt Solar Photovoltaic Demonstration Project.

The International Thermonuclear Experimental Reactor Program (ITER) is one of the world's largest projects of the International Science and Technology Cooperation Program. It is also the largest international science

This picture shows the signing ceremony of the Major Project Investment and Cooperation of the 2007 Hong Kong-Guangdong Economic, Technological Exchanges, and Trade Cooperation.

and technology project that China has taken part in. ITER has attracted the world's major nuclear countries and scientific and technological powers such as China, the European Union, India, Japan, South Korea, Russia, and the United States.

On November 21, 2006 at the Élysée Palace in Paris, France, after nearly five years of tough negotiations, the seven parties that participated in the ITER negotiation jointly signed the Agreement on Joint Implementation of the ITER Program to Build up the International Fusion Energy Organization, the Agreement on Joint Implementation of ITER Program to Build Privileges, and the Immunities of International Fusion Energy Organization, as well as other related documents. By then, ITER negotiations had been successfully concluded. On December 1, the Interim ITER International Organization was set up and ITER was formally founded.

In August 2007, the 29th Meeting of the 10th National People's Congress Standing Committee approved the Agreement on the Joint Implementation of ITER Program to Build up International Fusion Energy Organization, the Agreement on Joint Implementation of ITER Program to Build Privileges and Immunities of International Fusion Energy Organization. It marked the fact that China had completed the legal process of accessioning ITER. In October,

This picture shows the official signing ceremony of the ITER Agreement in November 2006 on Joint Cooperation Implementation and relevant documents, held at the Élysée Palace in Paris, France.

the ITER International Organization was formally launched. The technology assessment on ITER came to an end and participating countries launched their various procurement programs.

Galileo Program

The Galileo Program is the largest science and technology cooperation project between China and the European Union. The Galileo Program is an European civil satellite navigation program launched by the EU Commission and the European Space Agency. The purpose of the program is to build up a multipurpose and multifunctional civilian global satellite navigation positioning system that can cover the whole earth and is independent of the United States' global positioning and Russia's GLONASS system. Total investment reached €3.5 billion.

According to the cooperation agreement signed in 2003 by the People's Republic of China, the European Community, and its Member Countries on the Global Satellite Navigation System (Galileo Program), and the China National Remote Sensing Center and the European Galileo Program of the

Joint Implementation signed in 2005, China invested €200 million in the Galileo Program. Out of the total investment, €70 million is intended for the cooperation between the two parties in the development of the Galileo Program, and €130 million is invested for the deployment stage. China is the first non-EU country to participate in the Galileo Program.

The Human Genome Project

On July 7, 1999, the Human Genome Center of the Institute of Genetics of the CAS registered to participate in the Human Genome Project. In September, the International Collaborative Group accepted China's application and delineated the work scope for China—an area on the short arm of Human Chromosome 3. The core of the Human Genome Project is to construct a DNA sequence diagram. On April 15, 2003, leaders of the United States, United Kingdom, Japan, France, Germany, and China jointly issued the Joint Statement of Six Heads of Government on the Completion of the Human Genome Sequence Diagram, announcing the successful completion of the project. China's high-quality completion of its sequencing task in the Human Genome Program showed that China had achieved advanced international standards in genomics research.

Human Micro Genomics Program

The Human Micro Genomics Program is another major international genome-sequencing project after the Human Genome Project. The objective of the program is to determine the sequence of symbiotic microorganisms in the human body and to study gene functions that concern human growth and health.

In October 2005, delegates from 13 countries including the United States, Brazil, France, Germany, the United Kingdom, Japan, and China attended the First Coordination Meeting of the Human Micro Genomics Program. In 2006, China and France initiated the China–France Human Metagenome Group Cooperation. With the accession of other European countries, this cooperation has been reframed as the China–EU Cooperation in Human Microbial Groups. In December 2007, the founding meeting of the International League of Human Micro Genomes Groups was held in the United States in Washington D.C.

E-XFEL and FAIR Science Projects

The European Free Electron Laser Synchrotron Project (E-XFEL) and Ions and Anti-Proton Accelerator Project (FAIR) are two major construction projects for basic scientific research facilities in Germany. The total investment in

E-XFEL is €1.085 billion, and that for FAIR is €1.15 billion. Since November 2005, when China and Germany signed the Preparatory Phase Memorandum of Understanding on Participation in E-XFEL and FAIR, relevant institutes from China have actively taken part in the two science projects.

The Institute of High Energy Physics of the CAS and Peking University have actively participated in the E-XFEL project. The Institute of Modern Physics of the CAS has been made the coordinator of the FAIR project in China. It is also responsible for constructing the magnet and vacuum system of the cumulative rings and superconducting separation spectrometer.

Apart from these programs, China has made much progress as a leader of the International Human Liver Proteome Project, and other important international science programs and projects in which it is a participant. Some examples are the International Continental Scientific Drilling Program, the Global Change Research Program, the Global Earth Observation System, the International Integrated Ocean Drilling Program, the Hydrogen Economy International Partner Program, and the Large Hadrons Collider.

INDEX